New Trends in Asset Management

Enrica Bolognesi

New Trends in Asset Management

From Active Management to ESG and Climate Investing

palgrave
macmillan

Enrica Bolognesi
Department of Economics
and Statistics
University of Udine
Udine, Italy

ISBN 978-3-031-35056-6 ISBN 978-3-031-35057-3 (eBook)
https://doi.org/10.1007/978-3-031-35057-3

This Palgrave Macmillan imprint is published by the registered company Springer Nature Switzerland AG
The registered company address is: Gewerbestrasse 11, 6330 Cham, Switzerland

Contents

List of Figures

List of Tables

CHAPTER 1

Introduction

Abstract This chapter provides an overview of the topics covered in this book. The book is structured into seven chapters. We start with the first investment strategies that have characterised the asset management industry, typically based on diversification and on the manager's skills to select the best investment opportunities. Since then, academic research and the asset management industry have actively influenced each other by creating ever more sophisticated products and tools suitable for investors more involved in financial market trends. This path traverses the themes of the importance of the benchmark's construction methodologies and passive investing that have experienced an extraordinary evolution to move ever closer to the active management schemes. Finally, the emphasis is placed on the issue of sustainable finance and the tools used by managers to offer investment products committed to the fight against climate change.

Keywords Asset management industry · Benchmark · Active and passive management · Sustainable finance

This book aims at describing the evolution of the asset management industry over time, aiming to integrate two different perspectives, that of academic research and that of institutional investors. Academics and

E. Bolognesi, *New Trends in Asset Management*,
https://doi.org/10.1007/978-3-031-35057-3_1

asset managers have contributed to the evolution of this industry by creating increasingly intertwined common paths that are stimulus for the progress of the other. In fact, retracing the most important steps of this evolution, we realise that, on the one hand, empirical research has had a substantial impact, suggesting and stimulating portfolio allocations with increasingly evolved risk and return profiles. On the other hand, asset managers have been able to quickly integrate the results of academic research, launching ever new investment strategies and products to broaden their offer. Observing this evolution, we focus on traditional asset management products, i.e., mutual funds, because they are created for retail investors and, therefore, for whom collective asset management was born. In fact, mutual funds allow small investors to pool their money and benefit from diversification and from the expertise of professional asset managers.

The asset management industry has been developing since the 1970s; portfolio allocation was mainly based on the principle of financial diversification introduced by Markowitz in the 1950s. With the Capital Asset Pricing Model (CAPM) and its subsequent evolutions, asset managers have started to try to identify the 'market portfolio', i.e., the optimal, efficient, and desirable portfolio on which to base their asset allocation. Given the unrealistic opportunity of creating a portfolio that contains all investable assets, the choice shared by the industry has been to associate market indices with the concept of an optimal market portfolio. In addition, a choice that had a significant impact on asset allocation has been the use of the benchmark for risk and performance assessment, a tool that has assumed ever-increasing importance.

For these reasons, Chapter 2 focuses on the role of the benchmark in the asset management and on some alternative index construction methodologies. Cap-weighting, the most commonly used methodology, leads to portfolio allocations that favours large-cap stocks, in the belief that the firms' size can be used as a proxy of its representativeness in the reference market. While, on the one hand, this approximation is plausible and easy to implement, on the other it generates distortion effects that can impact negatively both on financial markets and on portfolio diversification. In fact, when we assist in decreasing investors' risk premiums, large flows of savings are quickly channelled towards mutual funds and, thus, mainly to large caps, since they show higher weights in the benchmarks. This can lead to an upward spiral in the prices and stock valuations, favouring speculative bubbles, such as the well-known *.com bubble*. As far as diversification is concerned, the risk is that the weight of these stocks becomes so high that they represent an excessively large portion of the overall market index, sacrificing the weight of the other components. We therefore focus on alternative index design methodologies, based both on the representativeness of the index components and on the efficiency of the portfolio. A comparison of the risk-return profile of these indices is provided, emphasising the differences.

Chapter 3 focuses on active management being the oldest investment philosophy. The aim is to underline the advantages and disadvantages of active portfolio management being the strategy based on the research of the creation of value for the investor through active choices. Active bets, meant as deviations from the benchmark composition, should allow for excess returns able, at least, to compensate the management fees applied to the fund. Academic research has emphasised many of the problems affecting active management being based on the expectations of asset managers on market trends or on their ability in stock picking. Indeed, because active management is the result of human choices, academic literature has emphasised some behavioural bias affecting portfolio managers. In addition, the performance statistics for active funds have been disappointing over time as a very small percentage of asset managers has demonstrated the ability to beat the market.

Chapter 4 focuses on an important evolution in active management called factor investing. In particular, the aim here is to describe the evolution of the academic research from the CAPM towards multi-factor models, with a particular emphasis on the three-factor model of Fama and French of 1993. This multi-factor pricing model has had a significant impact on the overall asset management industry; just consider that the two factors that we know today as the first investment styles in equity management were born from it, namely size and value. Hence the birth of factor investing in asset management, that involves selecting stocks based on their exposure to specific factors or characteristics, rather than simply buying a diversified portfolio of stocks. Empirical research has demonstrated that factors are persistent and pervasive drivers of return. The basic idea behind the factor investing is to identify securities that exhibit strong exposure to a particular factor and to construct a portfolio that is overweight in those securities. In particular, factor investors use quantitative techniques to identify factors that are expected to generate excess returns, but do not rely on individual security selection or market timing to achieve these returns. Instead, they aim to capture the systematic and persistent returns associated with certain factors over time. The implementation and diffusion of this investment strategy have been supported by the creation of factor indices to be used as benchmarks. Thus, we observe the characteristics of the main indices supporting factor investing. From the asset manager's perspective, factor investing is a sort of middle ground between passive and active management.

Chapter 5 continues in this direction showing the persistent marked intersection between active and passive management. The first part is dedicated to the description of the exponential growth of passive management supported by the growing preference of investors towards this industry. We focus on the birth of the Index Funds and the Exchange-Traded Funds (ETFs), providing several statistics on the asset under management flowing to passive investing, especially considering the equity markets. ETFs have indisputably become a leading form of investment and are greatly appreciated among investors thanks to their simplicity. In fact, they are low-cost, comprehensive, diversified portfolios and able to permit an exposure to various market segments. Moreover, they can be traded on an intraday basis. As highlighted, active management suffers from some difficult challenges such as investing in active funds seems to have 'little economic sense' especially if the returns are evaluated with respect to a market index. This statement is supported by the fact that, operationally, the adoption of a benchmark has the effect of anchoring the asset manager to the benchmark composition due to a multitude of technical and psychological factors. The close link existing between the fund and the benchmark, therefore, determines a substantial flattening of the portfolio's composition towards its benchmark. The perception by investors of generalised semi-passive management, which effectively does not allow for the achievement of sufficient overperformance to repay the management costs, helps to explain the strong growth in the volumes invested in passive funds. In other words, what we have witnessed has been a progressive disaffection of investors towards active funds. The next step of the industry has been the launch of hybrid products such as Smart beta ETFs, following rules-based investment strategies that seek to capture specific factors or characteristics that are believed to drive returns. Furthermore, the latest products born, which effectively has crossed the line between active and passive management are Active ETFs. It follows that, rather than a black-and-white choice, active management is getting more passive, and passive is getting more active.

Chapter 6 attempts to address the role and the growth of sustainable investments, nowadays a popular term that is meant to include all forms of socially responsible investing and ESG-oriented investing. Environmental Social and Governance integration means that these three factors are able to affect the investment decisions of financial analysts and portfolio managers. Accordingly, asset managers use ESG disclosure because of client demand or as part of their product development process. Proof of the large and growing market interest in the level of a company's degree of transparency about its ESG performance and policies is the exponential growth of assets under management that incorporates some element of ESG review and decision-making. Thus, we focus on the impact of the ESG disclosure scores on financial performance. Furthermore, we show the impact of regulation on disclosure, comparing the average scores of a broad sample of US and European firms.

Finally, the last chapter aims at addressing the new challenges of the asset management industry, i.e., ESG investing and, more recently, climate investing. If ESG investing is guided by the search for companies active on the three pillars, climate investing refers to the investment in companies, projects, and technologies that are focused on reducing the negative impact of climate change. Climate investing is an important part of the broader sustainable investing landscape, as it seeks to address one of the most pressing environmental challenges of our time. Climate investing is driven by the recognition that climate change poses significant risks to the global economy and society, and that urgent action is required to mitigate these risks. The investment community is increasingly focused on climate investing as a way to align financial returns with environmental and social goals. We firstly focus on the main ESG rating and their differences. ESG ratings often lack transparency in their calculation and differ substantially in the metrics on which they draw, as well as the methodologies used in their calculation, raising questions as to the extent to which their aggregation contributes to long-term value. Methodologies also tend to differ substantially across rating providers and result in a lack of correlation between ESG ratings supplied by different providers. Finally, we provide evidence of the growth of this new theme of investment, observing and describing the most recent ESG and climate indices launched.

CHAPTER 2

The Impact of Index Design on Asset Management

Abstract This chapter focuses on the impact of different equity index construction methodologies on the risk-return profile of managed portfolios. The first step is to define the characteristics that a market index must show to be used as benchmark in the asset management industry. Secondly, we critically analyse the main threats originated by using an equity market index composed according to the market cap of its components. The analysis of the impact of this methodology is extremely important because of their widespread use by institutional investors. In particular, the focus is on the distortions in their composition generated by overvalued securities (which can fuel financial bubbles) and on the risk of low diversification. Moreover, we provide evidence of the differences between alternative index construction methodologies, such as methodologies based on market representativity and on portfolio efficiency.

Keywords Benchmark · CAPM · Market portfolio · Index design · Cap-weighting

> Gains and losses that come with holding the benchmark portfolio are an 'act of God'.

E. Bolognesi, *New Trends in Asset Management*,
https://doi.org/10.1007/978-3-031-35057-3_2

> Gains and losses that come with deviation from the benchmark portfolio are an 'act of man'.
>
> (Clarke et al., 1994)

This statement summarises well the crucial role of the benchmark portfolio in asset management. We can see the benchmark acting as a pivot around which the portfolio manager constantly rotates, searching for value for the portfolio subscribers. In fact, the portfolio construction starts from the benchmark's composition and constantly develops around it. The benchmark establishes the absolute performance of the investment, the '*act of God*'; asset managers are responsible for the portfolio's relative performance, the '*act of man*', which is the result of the deviation of the managed portfolio from the benchmark. Its relevance has grown together with the exponential growth of the asset management industry worldwide. In fact, a reference parameter is required considering each aspect of portfolio management, from its construction and risk monitoring to the communication with subscribers. Thus, asset managers consider the benchmark as the *optimal portfolio*.

Since the 60s, the insights stemming from the Modern Portfolio Theory (Markowitz, 1952) and the Capital Asset Pricing Model (Lintner, 1965; Sharpe, 1964) have led to the consideration of the market portfolio as the mean–variance optimal portfolio. According to the CAPM, the entire market is one in which all risky assets, such as financial assets, consumer durables, real estate, and also non-traded assets like human capital are included. Thus, in reality, the market portfolio is unobservable and the possibility to test whether it is mean–variance efficient is also practically impossible. For this reason, the market portfolio is approximated by market indexes that represent a broad cross-section of the market. The most common approach is to use cap-weighted market indexes, (i.e., the S&P500 and the MSCI World) as proxies for the market portfolio. Cap-weighted market indexes are calculated by taking the market value of each company in the index and weighting it by its market capitalisation relative to the total market capitalisation of all companies in the index. Thus, cap-weighted market indexes overweight large-cap stocks and underweight small-cap stocks.

On the one hand, nowadays cap-weighted indexes have become an integral part of the investment process of long-term institutional investors such as mutual funds, pension funds, and insurance companies; it is a widely accepted methodology because it is a practical approach that allows for easy comparisons of investment performance against a market benchmark. On the other hand, the choice of an index is strategic because it has a critical impact on the portfolio construction, on the risks assumed, and, overall, on the final performance. Investors who seek to construct portfolios that are more representative of the true market portfolio may consider using alternative weighting schemes or broader market indexes that include a wider range of assets beyond traditional stocks and bonds. It is therefore worthwhile to dwell first on the characteristics that a market index must show in order to be a good benchmark and, hereafter, on alternative index construction methodologies.

What Is a (Good) Benchmark?

We define a benchmark as an index, composed with reference to commonly used financial indicators and developed by third parties. The benchmark is a basket of securities, representative of one or more markets or asset classes. Benchmarks must be aligned with the investment objectives and risks associated with the managed portfolio. Over time, the benchmark has increased its role as a communication vehicle between asset managers and subscribers of managed products.

Going into more detail on the role attributed to the benchmark, it is, above all, the portfolio that encloses the set of investable securities. The benchmark is usually a composite index, i.e., made up of several market indices in different proportions. For example, the benchmark for equity mutual funds is often composed of 95% of an equity market index and 5% of a money market index. The reason lies in the fact that, in this way, the portfolio maintains liquidity (in this case of 5%) to face significant redemptions. In the case of balanced portfolios, the composite benchmark consists of two or more indices representative of equity and bond markets.

From the asset manager's perspective, the benchmark is of primary importance in investment decisions, because it defines the origin point from which to measure the portfolio risk. This role is even more understandable if we consider that many portfolio managers are driven to leave the portfolio's absolute return in the background, because it is mainly rewarded according to the deviation from the benchmark (i.e., extra performance). Therefore, asset managers are led to evaluate their own operational choices on a relative base, in terms of parameters such as the tracking error volatility (i.e., the standard deviation of the portfolio's extra returns).

From the investors' perspective, a benchmark is a tool that allows, firstly, a historical performance comparison. Additionally, in the case of equity portfolios, the comparison of the portfolio with its benchmark is based on the geographical/sectorial composition. In case of bond portfolios, the comparison focuses mainly on the duration and the rating of the issues. From this comparison, it is possible to understand the deviations in the composition of the portfolio from its benchmark: these deviations represent *active bets*. Furthermore, the comparison with the benchmark is used for the calculation of incentive fees, if provided. This type of fee is applied if the performance exceeds that of the benchmark and is usually a percentage (typically 20%) of the excess return registered over a known time frame.

One of the key issues for a managed portfolio in embracing a market index as benchmark is its appropriateness. Generally, a market index requires the submission of several guidelines such as: (1) being *objective* and *transparent*, meaning that the benchmark should be clearly defined and easily understood. This means that the benchmark must be calculated by third parties, following rules that are not based on arbitrariness and are easily understandable: the financial community must also be aware of its composition and calculation rules, *ex ante*; (2) being *representative* of its asset class, meaning that it should define the range of eligible instruments specified by the investment targets; (3) being *replicable* and *investible*, meaning that each asset should be eligible instruments and tradable; (4) being computable and *developed from publicly available information*, meaning that investors should be able to monitor the benchmark portfolio and assess its exposures on a continuous basis.

The trade-off occurring between representativity and replicability is straightforward: the greater the representativity of the basket of securities (due to a wide number of assets included), the less achievable is the basket's replicability, due to the greater number of tradable assets and a feasible illiquidity risk. Similarly, the greater the number of index components, the higher the transaction costs supported by the financial portfolio. For instance, the Morgan Stanley Capital International (MSCI) World Index, is one of the most popular benchmarks of international equity funds, being composed of approximately 1500 stocks. The MSCI World Small Cap Index has about 4500 members. The complexity of investing and monitoring such a large number of assets is straightforward.

Focusing more in depth on representativity, this requirement is defined as the ability to reflect the characteristics of a specific market (i.e., the index components must reflect the investment opportunities available in its defined market). In operational terms, the industry has associated the representativeness of a firm with its size, choosing to focus on market-cap indexes. Market cap-weighting is supposed to describe and summarise a specific market, as larger firms assume higher weights on the index.

Cap-Weighting: *Pros* and *Cons*

As already mentioned, cap-weighting is justified by the Capital Asset Pricing Model and its central conclusion is that the cap-weighted portfolio of all available assets in the economy is a proxy of a mean–variance efficient portfolio. However, from an operational point of view, cap-weighted indexes are justified by their simplicity of use (both for replicability and transparency) even if, from a theoretical point of view, this choice has important implications. Using these indexes, investors should be aware that cap-weighted indexes omit most of the assets available in the economy, such as non-listed firms, social security, and private housing which are instead included in the theoretical market portfolio.

On the one hand, this simplification is balanced by several advantages that these indexes are able to offer. Firstly, usually market indexes are well known by investors and allow for a better understanding of the investable universe by the portfolio manager. Moreover, investors can diversify the portfolio in a simple and inexpensive way, simply by purchasing shares of the market portfolio, which will rebalance itself on a continuous basis as the prices of its individual components vary. At the same time, the index components are usually the largest caps in their market segment and among the most liquid, given the high correlation between size and liquidity. Finally, a further positive aspect of investing in cap-weighted indexes is the fact that they are characterised by low trading costs, given the passive nature of rebalancing deriving from the automatic adjustment of weights based on asset prices. Indeed, some rebalancing costs must also be incurred: at specific dates, some constituents are replaced with others that become significant enough to deserve to be included in the basket, or to completely eliminate some of the components following extraordinary events such as mergers and acquisitions or spin-offs.

On the other hand, the cap-weighted methodology leads to several drawbacks. Firstly, the investors' preference for a particular investment idea provokes a lower risk premium required by investors to hold the asset. Consequently, asset valuations sour as do their weights in the market index. Moreover, cap-weighting can be too concentrated on large caps, threatening the first aim of a market portfolio being representative and well diversified. These two important aspects deserve a more in-depth analysis.

Cap-Weighting and Financial Bubbles

The impact of cap-weighting on financial markets was clearly observed during the burst of the so-called *.com* bubble. It was this event that highlighted, for the first time in a straightforward way, the limitations of cap-weighting. In a nutshell, the fever for *.com* stocks led to excessive firms' valuations due to the expectation for exponential firms growth motivated by the new Internet era. Investors became overly enthusiastic about those stocks whose prices soared to unsustainable levels due to excessive speculation and positive sentiment.

Here it is worth retracing the experience of this financial bubble to highlight the repercussions of the cap-weighted methodology from an investor's perspective. The objective is to correlate the prices, weights, and valuations of stocks belonging to the Information Technology (IT) sector. To do this, we first look at Fig. 2.1, showing the performance of the sub-index, named S&P500 Information Technology Index, against the S&P500 Index, around the creation and the burst of the financial bubble.

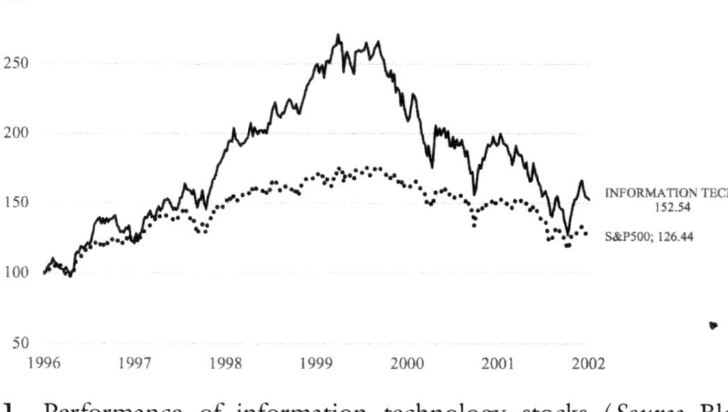

Fig. 2.1 Performance of information technology stocks (*Source* Bloomberg data. Author computation)

The outperformance of the internet sector, compared to the overall US equity market, favoured an increase in the weight of the related stocks, and components of the index. Figure 2.2 shows the trend of the IT sector's weight, within the overall S&P500 Index. It is easy to notice the impact of the outperformance of the IT sector on its weight, which has caused a sort of vicious circle between stock's prices and stock's weight. The graph shows that this weight has constantly and significantly grown during the late '90s, i.e., from 12.40% in December 1996 to 29.18% at the end of 1999. As a matter of fact, the first months of 2000 coincide with the peak of the 'irrational exuberance' as defined by the Federal Reserve Board chairman Alan Greenspan a few years earlier, in 1996. In the speech, Greenspan raised concerns about the stock market and the possibility that it was experiencing a bubble. He warned that investors were becoming overly optimistic and that their behaviour was not supported by the fundamentals of the economy.

The next step is to observe the relationship between weights and valuations of the index components. In particular, Fig. 2.3 shows the relationship between the average Price/Earnings ratio of each industry and its weight within the S&P500 Index. The analysis is focused on the three years before the Internet bubble burst (1997–1999). Observing the graph, we see that the IT sector is characterised by an average higher PE ratio with respect to the other industries. However, its valuation has achieved extremely high levels in 1999, due to huge prices compared to

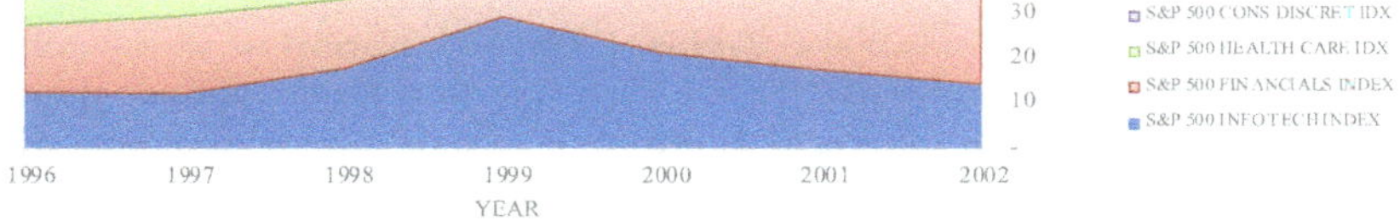

Fig. 2.2 Sectorial weights dynamics (*Source* Bloomberg data. Author computation)

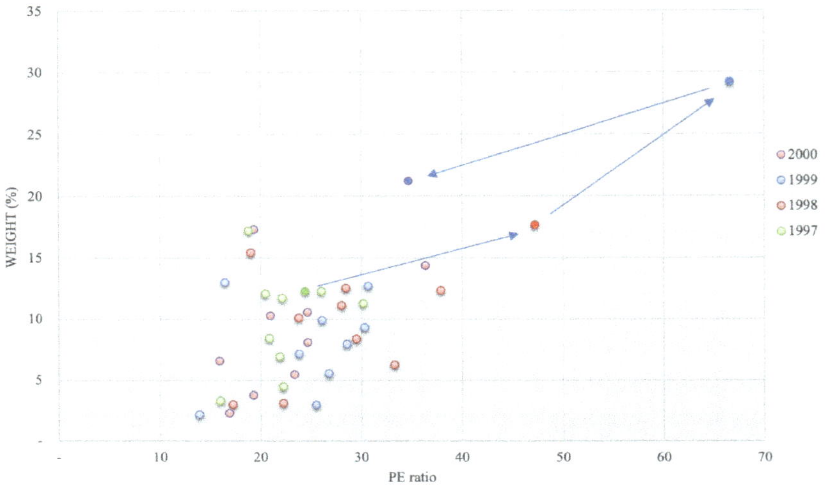

Fig. 2.3 Sectorial weights and price/earnings ratios (*Source* Bloomberg data. Author computation)

the firms' expected earnings. This overestimation has resulted in a proportional increase in the weights of these stocks into cap-weighted indexes. Therefore, portfolio managers have been 'forced' to constantly invest in these securities, also in the light of higher investors' appetite for risky assets during that period, to keep the portfolio's risk-return profile in line with the benchmark's one. These two conditions, growth of the flows into equity products and growth in their valuations, have led to an upward spiral of overvalued securities' weights.

Cap-Weighting and Diversification

Cap-weighted portfolios can also lead to a low diversification. In fact, one of the most evident drawbacks of the cap-weighted methodology is the high probability that large stocks become too heavily weighted into the index providing a portfolio which is too concentrated on larger securities. An example is the dynamic of the aggregate weight of the five largest and most popular technology companies, components of the Nasdaq 100 Index. These new high-growth stocks, known by the acronym FAANG, are: Meta (formerly known as Facebook); Amazon; Apple; Netflix; and

Fig. 2.4 FAANG stocks *vs* Nasdaq 100 Index (Market cap and weights of the FAANG vs Nasdaq 100 Index. *Source* Bloomberg Data. Author computation)

Alphabet (formerly known as Google). Figure 2.4 shows the relationship between the FAANG and the Nasdaq 100 Index. In particular, the first graph shows the dynamics of the aggregate market capitalisation of the FAANG as part of the Nasdaq 100 Index. The observation period is 10 years, starting from 2013, the year in which the term FAANG was coined. The FAANG market cap has increased from 915bn in 2013 to a maximum of 7trn in Q4 2021. The weight of the FAANG on Nasdaq 100 Index is shown in the second graph. It is striking to observe that the total weight of just five stocks (out of 100), has reached, on Q3 of 2020, the huge level of 42% of the Index.

Beyond Cap-Weighting: Alternative Index Weighting Schemes

Since capitalisation is a function of the stock market price, cap-weighted portfolios are to be considered optimal when the prices represent the securities' fair price and, therefore, when the hypothesis of market efficiency is verified. As already mentioned, although market indexes have been commonly accepted as the best proxy of the market, many critiques have been put forward that highlight the weaknesses of the CAPM. Among others, we recall Roll's critique about the impossibility of creating fully diversified portfolios. Roll (1977) argues that the CAPM is flawed because it is based on unrealistic assumptions about market conditions and investor behaviour. Specifically, Roll contends that the CAPM assumes that all investors have access to the same information and make investment decisions solely based on risk and return, without considering other factors such as market liquidity, taxes, or transaction costs.

He argues that investors have varying levels of information and may have different preferences or constraints that affect their investment decisions. As a result of these limitations, Roll suggests more sophisticated models, such as the Arbitrage Pricing Theory (APT), which allows for a wider range of variables and factors to be included in asset pricing, and may provide a more accurate representation of market behaviour.

A further critique of the CAPM comes from the Noisy Market Hypothesis, which was introduced by Fischer Black in 1986, who claims that market prices are not always efficient, but rather reflect the influence of noise traders who make investment decisions based on factors other than rational analysis of information. Black (1986) argues that this phenomenon can lead to short-term price movements that deviate from the true value of assets and may affect the ability of investors to make profits by trading on publicly available information. Similarly, Siegel (2006) argues that the market portfolio as defined by Modern Portfolio Theory is unrealistic and not representative of the actual market. In reality, there are many assets that are not included in the market portfolio, such as private equity, real estate, and commodities. Moreover, the weights of assets in the market portfolio are determined by their market value, which can be distorted by factors such as speculation and market bubbles. As an alternative, Siegel proposes the concept of a 'super portfolio' that includes all investable assets, both public and private, and weighs them based on their economic importance. This approach, he argues, would provide a more accurate representation of the market and a better foundation for portfolio management.

Consistently, stock market prices tend to deviate from their fair values creating mispricings. Hsu (2006) argues that stock prices are inefficient, meaning that underpriced stocks show a smaller market cap with respect to fair value and, vice versa, overpriced stocks gain a larger capitalisation. In other words, a cap-weighting scheme leads to a suboptimal portfolio strategy because portfolio weights are driven by market prices; as such, more weights are allocated to overvalued stocks and less weight to undervalued stocks. Therefore, these temporary shocks, called 'noise', can obscure the real value of securities and lead to an incorrect valuation, potentially for many years. In the academic literature, the phenomenon of price distortions has long been debated. Some studies have verified that the most popular stocks or investment topics, in a given period, are those that have shown the best past performance and, with high probability, are those with the highest valuations compared to their historical average. This phenomenon can also be observed at an institutional level where portfolio managers, motivated by constant comparison with other managers (specialising in the same market segment), and by objectives linked to relative performance with respect to the market index adopted, can tend towards imitative behaviour in investment choices, also known as herding.

As already shown, focusing on the Internet bubble, the homogeneity in the preferences of the economic operators inevitably gives rise to the effect of provoking excesses of optimism or pessimism, due to the concentration of investments and disinvestments on the same market topic and, therefore, on the same securities. The result is an upward spiral of the market valuations of these assets, which increases their weight within the market indices. As a result, overvalued stocks outweigh undervalued stocks, fuelling the bias. For these reasons, an increasing number of alternative market index construction methodologies have been promoted, in order to build more efficient portfolios, in terms also of a higher level of adherence of the market portfolio to the real economy, as well as greater diversification and a better risk-return profile.

Among these, Arnott, Hsu, and Moore developed in 2005 a methodology known as *fundamental indexation*, suggesting the creation of indices based on the accounting data of companies rather than on their market value. These authors, recognised as pioneers of this methodology, argue that it aimed at capturing the shares' intrinsic value and overcoming the problems arising from the 'noise trading' coming from irrational investors. In particular, they design a stock market index weighted on the basis of fundamentals, namely: revenues, book value, operating income, and dividends. Accordingly, they built a Composite Index, which weighs equally the average value of the four metrics. Their analysis is based on a sample of 1,000 US stocks from 1962 to 2004. Results provide evidence of an average annual excess return of 1.91% of the Composite Index over the Standard and Poor's 500 index associated with a similar risk profile. Thereafter, other studies provide evidence of the fundamental indexation superiority, focusing on different equity markets and time frames (see Bolognesi and Pividori (2016) for a literature review).

This methodology has been the subject of numerous critiques. The first claims that fundamental indexation is nothing more than a variant of a 'value' approach, already known in literature. The second critique is that the outperformance of the fundamental indices is recorded only during periods characterised by market anomalies such as financial bubbles, since at those times there are the most pronounced gaps between prices and earnings. In the asset management industry, fundamental indexes have been developed; the most famous is provided by Research Affiliates, a company founded in 2002 by Arnott himself.

Moving to other alternative index design, Amenc et al. (2011) identify two sets of indexes: those based on representativeness and those based on efficiency. In the first set, they recognise the *cap-weighted* and *fundamental-weighted* methodologies. The cap-weighted methodology uses the size in terms of market cap as a proxy for representativeness, while the fundamental approach weights firms in terms of the soundness of their balance sheets. Methodologies based on efficiency adopt a strategy consistent with the principles of portfolio theory, suggesting the search for securities characterised by the highest risk-return profile. *Equal-weighted*, *minimum volatility-weighted*, and *efficient-weighted* indexes fall into this category. In brief, equal-weighting attributes the same importance to each security, regardless of their characteristics. Therefore, they follow the so-called naive diversification, i.e., the rule of 1 out of n, which is independent of any components' characteristics. On the one hand, their performance is quite easy to calculate, being the arithmetic mean of each component's return. Moreover, if we consider a high number of members, we benefit from a higher diversification because it prevents larger caps to assume excessive weightings in the index. On the other hand, managing an equal-weighted portfolio is more costly as a rebalancing of all components is required at specific dates. In fact, over time, the outperforming stocks gain an increasing weight within the index, and vice versa for underperforming stocks. A periodic rebalancing of the index is, therefore, necessary and consists of the partial sale of the stocks that have outperformed and the purchase of the stocks that have underperformed, in order to provide an equal weight. As a result, the index rebalancing follows an implicit contrarian strategy, because winning stocks are sold to buy the losers in the belief, based on the mean-reversion hypothesis, that asset prices and historical returns gradually move towards the long-term mean.

Proceeding with efficiency-based indices, the *minimum volatility* methodology aims at minimising volatility and is based on the stocks' volatilities and correlations. According to this approach, no estimate of the expected returns of the components is necessary, therefore the focus is not on the risk-return profile but solely on risk minimisation. Finally, efficient-weighted indexes base their composition on the portfolio optimisation process. The objective, in this case, is to maximise the Sharpe Ratio. In this case, the composition of the index is based on estimates of expected return, volatility, and correlation between components.

The comparison between these five indexes allows for a greater understanding of their characteristics. Following Amenc et al. (2011) methodology, we have focused on the US equity market and, in particular, on the following indexes: S&P500 Index (cap-weighted); S&P500 Equal (equal-weighted); FTSE EDHEC-Risk Efficient Index (efficient-weighted); MSCI Minimum Volatility Index (minimum volatility weighted); FTSE RAFI 1000 Index (fundamental weighted). Each index is a total return, meaning that dividends are considered in the performance. The analysis period is twenty years, from January 2003 to January 2023. Figure 2.5 shows the 20-year pattern of the selected indexes. Overall, the equity market has registered a positive return: the best performer has been the efficient index followed by the equal-weighted index. The worst performer has been the minimum volatility, followed by the cap-weighted.

Table 2.1 reports the main statistics. It is worth dwelling on some of the results. The data highlight, over the selected period, an extra

Fig. 2.5 Performance of alternative US equity market indexes (2003–2023) (*Source* Bloomberg data. Author computation)

performance of almost all non-cap-weighted indexes. The exception is the minimum volatility that shows a lower return with respect to the S&P 500 Index as well as the overall lowest volatility. Moving to the risk-adjusted measure, the efficient index presents the highest Sharpe Ratio (0.62) while fundamental and cap-weighted show the lowest (0.56). The beta parameter, calculated in relation to the S&P 500 Index, confirms the defensive structure of the minimum volatility index. On the opposite side, the most aggressive index is the equal weighted (beta equal to 1.1).

The risk-return profiles of the analysed indexes can be observed in Fig. 2.6. The graph provides evidence that dominant portfolios are the minimum volatility and the efficient portfolio. The cap-weighted shows a medium volatility with respect to the others and it is dominated by the efficient portfolio. In fact, if we had focused on the risk profile relative to the cap-weighted index, we could have obtained a better result by combining the investment in the risk-free asset and the efficient portfolio.

Overall, we can conclude that the different index construction methodologies lead to significantly different results in terms of risk-return profile. Over the time horizon analysed, the cap-weighted index shows an average risk profile compared to the other indexes. The strength of this index is, as mentioned several times, the absence of the need to periodically rebalance its components. Instead, all the other indexes require a periodic rebalancing and, therefore, a greater turnover which could weigh down the

Table 2.1 Return characteristics of alternative index construction methodologies (2003–2023)

	Cap-weighted	*Fundamental weighted*	*Equal weighted*	*Efficient weighted*	*Min volatility weighted*
Return	9.88%	10.79%	11.49%	11.48%	9.08%
Standard deviation	17.65%	19.19%	19.89%	18.47%	15.14%
Sharpe ratio	0.56	0.56	0.58	0.62	0.60
Minimum	−20.02%	−21.79%	−20.67%	−20.57%	−19.34%
Maximum	11.46%	13.83%	14.44%	14.30%	12.24%
Beta (vs CW)	1	1.06	1.1	1.02	0.81

Analyses are based on weekly returns. Returns and standard deviations are annualised. Beta is relative to the cap-weighted index

Source Bloomberg data. Author computation

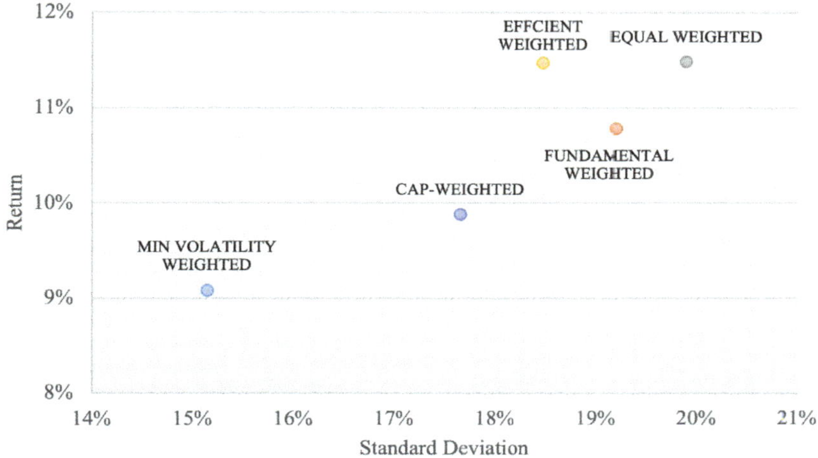

Fig. 2.6 Risk-return profile of alternative index construction methodologies (2003–2023) (Analyses are based on weekly returns. Returns and standard deviations are annualised. *Source* Bloomberg data. Author computation)

costs borne by the portfolio and, in the case of large portfolios, have an impact on stock prices.

References

Amenc, N., Goltz, F., Martellini, L., & Ye, S. (2011). *Improved beta? A comparison of index-weighting schemes*. EDHEC-Risk Institute.

Black, F. (1986). Noise. *The Journal of Finance, 41*(3), 528–543.

Bolognesi, E., & Pividori, M. (2016). Fundamental indexation in Europe: New evidence. *Journal of Financial Management, Markets and Institutions, 4*(2), 103–128.

Clarke, R. G., Krase, S., & Statman, M. (1994). Tracking errors, regret, and tactical asset allocation. *Journal of Portfolio Management, 20*(3), 16–24.

Hsu, J. C. (2006). Cap-weighted portfolios are sub-optimal portfolios. *Journal of Investment Management, 4*(3), 1–10.

Lintner, J. (1965). The valuation of risky assets and the selection of risky investments in stock portfolios and capital budgets. *Review of Economics and Statistics, 47*, 13–37.

Markowitz, H. M. (1952). Portfolio selection. *Journal of Finance, 7*(1), 77–91.

Roll, R. (1977). A critique of the asset pricing theory's tests part I: On past and potential testability of the theory. *Journal of Financial Economics, 14*(2), 129–176.

Sharpe, W. F. (1964). Capital asset prices: A theory of market equilibrium under conditions of risk. *Journal of Finance, 19*(3), 425–442.

Siegel, J. (2006, June 14). The noisy market hypothesis. *Wall Street Journal*, A14.

CHAPTER 3

Pros and Cons of Active Management

Abstract This chapter focuses on the benefits and on the threats of active management retracing the most significant contributions of the extensive literature on this topic. We firstly focus on the definition of active management, active risk and on the sources of alpha. Then we focus on the main issues of interest concerning active management, namely: (1) the higher costs and underperformance of active funds compared with respect to index funds; (2) the attitude of herding which can generate market inefficiencies; (3) the impact of the incentive schemes, short-terminism, and incentive fees on returns; (4) the threats and opportunities of mispricing and market anomalies.

Keywords Active management · Herding · Incentive schemes · Behavioural managers

We firstly can define active management as where there are active human decisions being made about what the portfolio buys and what the portfolio sells. The term active management refers to the implementation of strategies which involve one or more deviations of the portfolio components' weights with respect to the benchmark. Here we rely on the definition provided by Siegel (2003):

E. Bolognesi, *New Trends in Asset Management*, https://doi.org/10.1007/978-3-031-35057-3_3

> Active management can be viewed as taking active bets against a benchmark. In other words, each security in the benchmark can be held at the benchmark weight (which represents no active risk) or at a greater or lesser weight (which represents some active risk). You can also take active risk by holding securities that aren't in the benchmark. Thus, any active portfolio can be understood as an index fund plus a portfolio of long and short positions relative to the benchmark. (p. 32)

In more detail, the active risk is measured by the excess returns volatility of a managed portfolio compared to its benchmark (the active returns). It is therefore natural to expect that a manager who takes no active positions (who holds the benchmark portfolio) will have no active returns and no active risk. In this regard, Grinold (1989) identifies the factors that influence the managers' ability to generate extra returns. His model, known as the *Fundamental Law of Active Management,* is based on three variables: the ability of the manager (skill), the frequency with which investment opportunities can be identified (breadth), and the added value of the strategy adopted:

> You can think of breadth as how often you play (number of times per year) and skill as a measure of how well you play. The value added will be measured in terms of annual return. A strategy's value added will be proportional to the strategy's Sharpe ratio. (Grinold, 1989, p. 30)

Thus, active management means that the holding weights differ from the benchmark portfolio in an attempt to produce excess risk-adjusted returns, also known as *alpha*. The different holding weights reflect management's differing expectations of the overall market. In addition, the manager must achieve excess returns systematically and with a reasonable deviation from the benchmark. Only in these circumstances active management is defined as efficient. Active managers make investment decisions based on a variety of factors, including economic conditions, company financials, and industry trends, and may buy or sell securities frequently to try to capture market opportunities. Their approach may be strictly algorithmic, entirely discretionary, or somewhere in between.

On the other side, passive management has been born as the simple replication of a market index. Passive management is based on the Efficient Market Hypothesis, meaning that asset managers are unable to systematically outperform the benchmark or that any excess returns are so low as not to justify the higher costs that active management involves (costs of negotiation, analyses, research, etc.). Thus, passive managers do not seek any other return than the market's. Accordingly, they build portfolios that reflect some benchmarks, without the need of generating excess return. The turnover is usually low as are negotiation and management fees. As a consequence, passive management is significantly cheaper than active management.

The comparison between active and passive management has been at the centre of an academic debate for a long time. Although the empirical evidence acknowledges the difficulty of benchmark comparisons, the asset management industry emphasises the following advantages that investors may consider in investing in active funds: *(i) Potential for outperformance*: active management may provide an opportunity for skilled managers to identify undervalued or mispriced securities, anticipate market trends, and generate higher returns than the broader market. *(ii) Flexibility*: active management allows for more flexibility in portfolio management, as the manager can adjust the portfolio holdings based on market conditions, economic outlook, and other factors. This flexibility can potentially lead to better risk management and higher returns. *(iii) Diversification:* active managers can provide investors with access to a wider range of investment opportunities and asset classes that may not be available through passive strategies. This can help investors to diversify their portfolios and potentially improve risk-adjusted returns. *(iv) Customisation:* active managers can tailor their investment strategies to meet the specific needs and objectives of individual investors or clients. This customisation can provide investors with greater control over their portfolios and help them to achieve their unique investment goals.

Focusing on the main of these issues, Fuller (1998) identifies 'informational advantages' as one potential *source of alpha* in investment management. He notes that managers who have access to unique or proprietary information, or who are able to process information more quickly or effectively than others, may be able to generate alpha. More specifically, he focuses on possible management approaches which are potentially capable of generating value:

1. *Superior (private) information*. This approach is based on the possibility of producing better information than that which is publicly available. This information is the result of analysis by the manager based on the fundamentals of the companies being invested. Those who use this style are defined as traditional (or *fundamental*)

managers because they are characterised by their forecasting skills regarding the earnings or profitability of listed companies.

2. *Process information better*. This means having quantitative forecasting models capable of processing information in a better way than those produced by the average investors on the market. In this case, managers who follow this approach are referred to as *quantitative*.

Stating that an active investor has superior information compared to other operators does not imply that the market forms expectations in a distorted way. Instead, it is understood that the investments are based on private information that the market does not possess and therefore that it is unable to process, either correctly or distortedly. Similarly, if the model the market uses to process information is not the most efficient, then it is possible that the expectations embedded in the prices are not biased, but simply not as accurate as those that could be generated by a better model. The criticism that Fuller poses to these two methodologies can be summarised in a simple question: what is the probability that an individual investor (even a professional one) is able to gather superior information or to develop a better model than the market when there are many other subjects who try to do the same? The answer provided by Fuller is a third management approach, based on the search for market anomalies caused by behavioural mistakes:

3. *Behavioural Biases*. This approach is based on the irrationality in the investment choices of economic agents which is reflected in the market prices. Portfolio managers, therefore, concentrate on the search for shares that are not fairly priced as a consequence of the cognitive biases of market participants. Thus, *behavioural managers* try to identify mispriced securities caused by behavioural distortions. Among these, the most common is attributable to the presence of professional investors who do not operate in compliance with traditional finance models and are affected by heuristics (such as loss aversion). These behaviours induce managers to fall into mental mistakes in a systematic way.

The generation of extra returns is linked to the alignment of investors' and portfolio managers' interests. As regards the active risks, several constraints are set by the risk management in terms of deviation of the managed portfolio from the benchmark. The primary objective of the risk manager is to keep a level of risk assumed by managers in line with the degree of risk that the shareholders of the asset management company deem 'desirable'. The metric commonly used to assess the intensity of active bets is the *tracking error volatility*. It is calculated as the standard deviation of the daily or weekly extra returns of the portfolio on its benchmark. It follows that the greater the tracking error volatility, the higher the active risk, and, consequently, the intensity of active management. The measure commonly used to define active management is the *information ratio* defined as the ratio between the average excess returns of the portfolio and the tracking error volatility. The information ratio allows testing whether a portfolio managed by a fund provides a return significantly larger than the benchmark. Since the benchmark portfolio is supposedly efficient, the information ratio is useful in evaluating the fund manager's skills; the greater, the better the manager's ability to select profitable investment opportunities.

Main Issues in Active Management

Higher Costs and Underperformance

As already mentioned, active management is characterised by higher fees and expenses than passive management strategies, such as index investing. These higher costs can eat into investment returns and make it more difficult to achieve long-term investment goals.

There is a vast literature that focuses on the performance recorded by active managers. Most of these studies highlight the poor results that can arise from an active management approach (*'act of man'*) compared to both market indices (*'act of God'*) and passively managed funds. Focusing on the most cited literature on active returns and performance persistence, we can go back to the late 60s, when the first works on this subject were published. To sum up the main evidence, we firstly recall Jensen (1968) arguing that mutual funds do not outperform the market on a risk-adjusted basis. Fama (1970) focuses on the efficient market hypothesis (EMH), which posits that markets are generally efficient and that it is difficult for investors to consistently outperform the market. Malkiel (1973) claims that markets are generally efficient, and that it is difficult for active managers to consistently outperform the market. Sharpe (1991) demonstrates that, in the aggregate, the managers of mutual funds do not record higher returns than the benchmark. The reason behind this statement lies in the fact that active management, in reality, is nothing more than a 'zero-sum game'. Carhart (1997) finds that past performance is a good predictor of future performance, but only for a small subset of funds. Moreover, outperformance is largely due to luck rather than skill.

Some evidence shows that the generalised underperformance recorded by active funds is justified by the presence of transaction costs which affect exclusively the performance of the managed portfolios. In other words, the difficulty encountered when there is competition between a fund and a market index can be attributed to the characteristic of the benchmark which represents a 'paper portfolio' (Frino & Gallaher, 2001). More evidence has been provided about the limited persistence over time of the outperformance of active funds. This means that it is rare to find a manager that can claim consistency in alpha generation (Davis, 2001).

Cremers and Petajisto (2009) introduced the concept of 'active share', which measures the degree to which a portfolio deviates from its benchmark index, and have found that funds with high active share outperform their benchmarks. Fama and French (2010) examined the relative importance of skill and luck in mutual fund performance and found that most of the variation in returns can be attributed to luck rather than skill. Pastor and Stambaugh (2012) examined the performance of mutual funds as they grow in size. They found that, as funds become larger, their performance tends to decline. Dyck et al. (2013) examined the performance of active mutual funds in 32 countries over a 15-year period. The authors found that active management tends to underperform passive management in most countries, but that there are some countries (such as Japan and the United Kingdom) where active management has been more successful.

To sum up, the percentage of active managers who beat their benchmark varies from year to year, but research has consistently shown that a minority of active managers outperform their respective benchmarks over the long term.

Recent statistics provided by the industry confirm these results. According to the S&P Dow Jones Indices Research (2021), which tracks the performance of actively managed mutual funds in the United States, the percentage of active funds that outperformed their respective benchmarks in 2020 ranged from 9.83 to 39.41%, depending on the asset class and time period analysed. Over longer time periods, the percentage of active funds that outperform their benchmarks tends to decrease. The latest report, published in June 2021, found that over a 1-year period, 50.8% of large-cap funds, 57.5% of mid-cap funds, and 72.7% of small-cap funds underperformed their benchmarks. Over a 5-year period, the figures were even worse, with 81.8% of large-cap funds, 88.6% of mid-cap funds, and 94.6% of small-cap funds underperforming their benchmarks. Similarly, the 'Active/Passive Barometer' provided by Morningstar found that only 25% of actively managed funds in the United States beat their respective category average over the 10-year period ending in December 2020.

This evidence highlights the difficulty of active management in creating value for the subscriber. Here it is necessary to dwell also on the operational flexibility granted to managers. An indispensable requirement for achieving extra returns with respect to the benchmark is, obviously, the manager's ability to implement active bets on the portfolio he manages. However, the operational flexibility of the manager is frequently constrained by the risk management within certain risk parameters aimed at safeguarding the managed portfolio. In other words, risk budgets are generally set by risk managers in relation to the benchmark. The manager's freedom of action is therefore limited in order to avoid deviations that are too extreme and which could compromise the performance of the managed portfolio and, therefore, the reputation of the asset management company.

Herding Behaviour

One of the major threats to active managers is 'herding'. Herding refers to the behaviour of investors or traders who follow the actions of their peers, rather than making decisions based on their own independent analysis and information. This behaviour can result in a group of investors making similar investment decisions, leading to increased buying or selling pressure and potentially causing market inefficiencies. Herding behaviour can be driven by a number of factors, such as a desire to conform to social norms, a fear of missing out on potential profits, and a perception of safety in numbers. In some cases, herding can be rational and driven by a desire to benefit from the collective wisdom of the group. However, herding can also be irrational and lead to market bubbles and crashes, where investors all follow the same strategy without regard to fundamental factors.

The most theoretical research focuses on the rational motivations that can push asset managers towards the same investment choices. More specifically, the incentive of a fund manager to herd can be explained by several issues. The first is a ***reputational risk***. In particular, the trigger for herding can be attributed to the willingness of asset managers to preserve or improve their reputation. Scharfstein and Stain (1990) suggest that when investment managers make unconventional investment decisions and deviate from the consensus, they may face negative feedback from their clients or peers if those decisions do not work out. As a result, investment managers may feel pressure to conform to the consensus and avoid deviating too far from the herd:

> A basic tenet of classical economic theory is that investment decisions reflect agents' rationally formed expectations; decisions are made using all available information in an efficient manner. A contrasting view is that investment is also driven by group psychology, which weakens the link between information and market outcomes. (p. 465)

This form of ***group psychology***, in many cases, generates the amplification of exogenous shocks on the markets. Lakonishok et al. (1992) found that mutual fund managers tend to overweight stocks that are widely held by other mutual funds, leading to a positive correlation between the performance of individual mutual funds. Bikhchandani et al. (1992) propose that herding behaviour can be driven by information cascades, where investors update their beliefs about the value of an investment based on the actions of others, rather than on their own information. However, they also note that information cascades can be inefficient, in that they can cause investors to ignore their own private information and to follow the actions of others without regard to fundamental factors. Devenow and Welch (1996) propose that herding behaviour can be rational or irrational depending on the circumstances. They suggest that herding can be rational in situations where investors have limited information and are uncertain about the value of an investment. In these situations, investors may be more likely to follow the actions of others as a way of reducing their uncertainty.

The empirical literature on herding is mainly based on the impact of herding on financial markets. One of the cornerstones of these studies is certainly the work of Grinblatt et al. (1995) focused on the analysis of the performance of a sample of 155 US mutual funds, in the time frame 1975–1984. The authors show the asset managers' attitude to the evaluation of securities on the basis of their past returns (positive-feedback trading). Their results reveal the managers' tendency to buy and sell the same securities at the same time with a frequency that cannot be attributed to pure chance. Froot et al (1992) show that investors tend to follow the actions of their peers, and that this behaviour is more prevalent during periods of high market uncertainty. Moreover, the study found that herding behaviour can have a significant impact on stock returns. Specifically, the authors found that stocks with high levels of herding tend to have higher volatility and lower returns. They argue that the short-term time horizon causes inefficiencies in financial markets. In particular, traditional models that assume long-term investment choices consider the presence of informational externalities as a negative factor. Conversely, in the short run, investors view these externalities as opportunities to be seized. They are thus led to base their decisions on this type of information rather than on the fundamental values of the observed assets. To sum up, '*speculators herd: they acquire "too much" of some types of information and "too little" of others*'. Falkenstein (1996) focuses on the common attitude of institutional investors towards particular categories of securities. In particular, the composition of US mutual funds suggests managers' aversion towards those securities is characterised by a low degree of liquidity (such as, for example, small-cap stocks). At the same time, managers favour stocks about which they have more information (even if of a public nature) and which boast the longest historical series. Avery and Chevalier (1999) conducted a study on mutual fund herding behaviour and found that mutual fund managers tend to herd together and follow the same investment strategies, particularly in periods of high market uncertainty. They suggest that herding behaviour can be influenced by the incentives facing mutual fund managers, such as performance-based fees and career concerns. Moreover, they show that more experienced fund managers have less incentive to imitate other managers. In this regard, the literature shows that the homogeneity in the investors' preferences can cause an excess of optimism or pessimism originating from the concentration of investment strategies on the same securities. For example, this phenomenon has been analysed by Sharma et al. (2006) focusing on the investment choices of managers related to Internet stocks before 2000. The study demonstrates a herding attitude of increasing intensity during the bullish phase that characterised the international stock markets. Moreover, they suggest that this herding behaviour can lead to market inefficiencies, as investors may overreact to news or market developments and drive asset prices away from their fundamental values.

Herding behaviour is an example of a behavioural finance phenomenon, where investors make decisions based on the actions of others rather than their own independent analysis and information. Menkhoff et al. (2006) argue that herding behaviour in financial markets can be explained by a combination of rational and behavioural factors. They suggest that rational factors such as information asymmetry, uncertainty, and risk aversion can lead to herd behaviour in financial markets. Additionally, they argue that behavioural factors such as social influence, conformity, and cognitive biases also play a significant role in herd behaviour. They also note that cognitive biases such as overconfidence, anchoring, and confirmation bias can lead to investors ignoring their own analysis and following the crowd.

Incentive Schemes and Short-Terminism

Incentive schemes are generally linked to the performance (sometimes risk adjusted) of the portfolio compared to its benchmark. In some cases, an additional target is set in terms of comparison with other funds of the same category/asset class. This dual target can significantly influence investment decisions inducing managers to get closer to other funds' allocations and, thus, generating homogeneous behaviour. In other words, the attention paid to the performance of peer funds can probably fuel the phenomenon of herding among fund managers of the same asset class.

Usually, portfolio managers are incentivised based on short-term performance metrics, such as quarterly or annual returns. This factor may also encourage herding behaviour, as managers may be more likely to follow the crowd in order to achieve short-term gains. From a psychological point of view, the moment in which the performance of the managed portfolio is recorded for the purpose of calculating the annual bonus is certainly relevant for a manager. This moment commonly coincides with the end of the year. The time horizon is an important element in portfolio management because it can cause distortions in the investment decisions of the managers by influencing their behaviour. For example, approaching maturity could change the manager's willingness to take risks. Another possible effect deriving from the approaching end of the year could manifest itself in the difficulty of implementing management strategies which require a long time horizon to be able to appreciate the effects.

Academic literature focuses on this issue. Froot et al. (1992) argue that short-term investment horizons can lead to suboptimal investment decisions and potentially harm long-term returns. In their study, they found that mutual fund managers with shorter investment horizons tended to trade more frequently and incur higher transaction costs, which led to lower net returns. They also found that managers with longer investment horizons tended to hold more concentrated portfolios and take more risks, which led to higher returns. They argue that short-term investment horizons can create a 'myopic' focus on short-term performance, which can lead to inefficient trading and suboptimal portfolio construction. They suggest that longer investment horizons can provide a more rational and disciplined approach to investing, allowing managers to take advantage of market inefficiencies and generate higher returns over the long term.

Chevalier and Ellison (1997) analyse the effects of incentive schemes (affected by the end-of-year time horizon) on the risk appetite of the manager. Their study demonstrates the greatest exposure to risk in conjunction with the last quarter of the year and this effect is amplified if we refer to the 'younger' funds. In detail:

> In line with popular wisdom, young funds appear to have an incentive late in the year to gamble and try to catch the market if they are a few points behind; they may also have an inventive to play it safe and act more like an index fund if they are ahead of the market. (p. 1170)

Baker (1998), through a survey involving sixty-four English fund managers, analyses the effects of performance monitoring on the behaviour of the manager. In particular, the author focuses on the risk attitude of the manager, on the reward system, and on the time horizon of investment decisions. Observing the implications of the frequency of monitoring the recorded performance results reveals an inverse proportionality with the time horizon of the manager's strategies. Another important negative relationship verified in this study is between the average permanence of a security in the portfolio and the percentage of the bonus linked to the relative performance of the managed product. The resulting effect is the presence of factors which concentrate the manager on short-termism and modifying the behaviour. Concretely, this translates into holding periods of the positions held in the portfolios that are lower than the optimal ones, with particular reference to equity investments.

Still focusing on incentive schemes, as far as returns are concerned, maximising the fund's return coincides with maximising the manager's remuneration. The mechanism most commonly used to achieve this goal is represented by *incentive fees* applied to managed portfolios. These fees are paid to the management company in case of the fund outperformance. Elton et al. (2003) analyse this issue, defining this type of fees as follows:

> An incentive fee is a reward structure that makes management compensation a function of investment performance relative to some benchmark. (…) There are a number of reasons why incentive fees are considered desirable. Perhaps the most often cited is that incentive fees align manager interest with investor interests. Both groups do better when investment does better. (p. 779)

The authors focus on a set of US funds charging incentive fees to verify the effects they generate on managers' behaviour. Their results confirm the literature showing a greater convexity in the structure of the incentives to managers in the presence of incentive fees. In other words, results show a higher tracking error that characterises the funds that apply incentive fees. Furthermore, the risk exposure exhibited by these funds is magnified in the time window following a period of disappointing performance. In line with these results, Massa and Patgiri (2008) find that incentive mechanisms induce managers to take on greater risks while reducing the probability of the fund's survival. The reason for the outperformance can be attributed both to lower fixed management fees (compensated by incentive fees) and to higher selection skills of managers (attributable to the fact that the best managers are attracted by companies able to offer more competitive incentive schemes). As a result, incentive fees are a desirable feature for fund subscribers.

Finally, several other studies have examined the impact of incentive schemes on active management. Here, it is worth mentioning Brown et al. (1996) argue that when the compensation is linked to relative performance, fund managers likely to end up as 'losers' will manipulate fund risk differently than those managing portfolios likely to be 'winners'. The authors focus on the performance of 334 growth-oriented mutual funds during 1976 to 1991 and demonstrate that mid-year losers tend to increase fund volatility in the latter part of an annual assessment period to a greater extent than mid-year winners. Furthermore, they show that this effect became stronger as industry growth and investor awareness of fund performance increased over time.

Mispricing, Market Anomalies, and Behavioural Managers

Behavioural finance contrasts with traditional economic models as it questions certain simplifying assumptions concerning the behaviour of economic agents. With reference to financial markets, behavioural finance considers how investors form their expectations about the future, and how these forecasts are incorporated into prices. The heuristics of individuals widely demonstrated in the literature (representativeness, availability, anchoring) and the biases to which investors are subject (overconfidence, excessive optimism, illusion of control) have the effect of influencing both operators' expectations and market prices, generating market anomalies.

Considering the vast literature on behavioural finance, we focus on the contributions that first highlighted the errors in the investment choices of market operators. For example, investors tend to sell 'winning' stocks too early and keep stocks that have exhibited a negative trend in their portfolio for too long (Shefrin & Statman, 1985), or excessive turnover of institutional portfolios (Trueman, 1988). Another habit that emerges from the literature is the preference of investors towards the purchase of securities that have distinguished themselves as winners in the past and the sale of the so-called losers (Hirshleifer et al., 1994), thus defining a behavioural attitude, in the medium-term long term, to be positive-feedback traders (De Long et al., 1990).

These distortions in investment choices are often interpreted as the product of some typical non-rational attitudes of economic operators. For example, excessive confidence in one's predictive abilities leads to underestimating the variability of events and therefore it is reflected in the risk appetite. Odean (1999) demonstrates how overconfidence is the cause of the excessive operations of some traders, which also result in high transaction costs such as to compromise the overall performance of the portfolio. Still in the literature, the tendency towards conservatism (Edwards, 1968) leads the investor to select, among the available information, those that confirm his or her hypotheses, ignoring the elements that call them into question. The resulting effect is anchoring to pre-established positions, with a consequent adverse selection of one's investments. In fact, investors, in making a judgment, are anchored to certain values that are impressed on their minds and do not deviate adequately from them. For example, Shefrin (2000), observing the work of financial analysts, notes that they start from an initial hypothesis in evaluating a company to which, however, they remain mentally linked even when processing new information.

On the one hand, portfolio managers, like all investors, can be subject to a range of behavioural biases, such as confirmation bias, overconfidence, and loss aversion. These biases can lead to herding behaviour and an over-reliance on consensus views. On the other hand, portfolio managers may concentrate on the search for shares that are not fairly priced as a consequence of the cognitive biases of market participants. Behavioural managers are investment managers who focus on identifying and exploiting behavioural biases and irrationalities in financial markets. They may use techniques such as sentiment analysis, social media monitoring, and quantitative analysis of investor behaviour in order to make investment decisions.

Some proponents of behavioural finance argue that incorporating a behavioural perspective into investment management can lead to better decision-making and improved returns. However, others argue that it is difficult to consistently generate alpha through behavioural strategies, and that these approaches may be subject to their own biases and limitations.

References

Avery, C. N., & Chevalier, J. A. (1999). Herding over the career. *Economics Letters, 63*(3), 327–333.

Baker, M. (1998). Fund managers' attitudes to risk and time horizons: The effect of performance benchmarking. *The European Journal of Finance, 4*, 257–278.

Bikhchandani, S., Hirshleifer, D., & Welch, I. (1992). A theory of fads, fashion, custom, and cultural change as informational cascades. *Journal of Political Economy, 100*(5), 992–1026.

Brown, K. C., Harlow, W. V., & Starks, L. T. (1996). Of tournaments and temptations: An analysis of managerial incentives in the mutual fund industry. *The Journal of Finance, 51*(1), 85–110.

Carhart, M. M. (1997). On persistence in mutual fund performance. *Journal of Finance, 52*(1), 57–82.

Chevalier, J., & Ellison, G. (1997). Risk taking by mutual funds as a response to incentives. *The Journal of Political Economy, 105*(6), 1167–1200.
Cremers, K. M., & Petajisto, A. (2009). How active is your fund manager? A new measure that predicts performance. *The Review of Financial Studies, 22*(9), 3329–3365.
Davis, J. (2001). Mutual fund performance and manager style. *Financial Analysts Journal, 57*(1), 19–26.
Devenow, A., & Welch, I. (1996). Rational herding in financial economics. *European Economic Review, 40*(3–5), 603–615. https://www.sciencedirect.com/science/article/abs/pii/0014292195000739.
De Long, J. B., Shleifer, A., Summers, L., & Waldmann, R. J. (1990). Positive feedback investment strategies and destabilizing rational expectations. *The Journal of Finance, 45*(2), 379–395.
Dyck, A., Lins, K. V., & Pomorski, L. (2013). Does active management pay? New international evidence. *The Review of Asset Pricing Studies, 3*(2), 200–228.
Edwards, W. (1968). Conservatism in human information processing. In B. Kleinmutz (Ed.), *Formal representation of human judgement*. New York.
Elton, E. J., Gruber, M. J., & Blake, C. R. (2003). Incentive fees and mutual funds. *The Journal of Finance, 58*(2), 779–804.
Falkenstein, E. (1996). Preferences for stock characteristics as revealed by mutual fund portfolio holdings. *The Journal of Finance, 51*, 111–135.
Fama, E. F. (1970). Efficient capital markets: A review of theory and empirical work. *The Journal of Finance, 25*(2), 383–417.
Fama, E. F., & French, K. R. (2010). Luck versus skill in the cross-section of mutual fund returns. *The Journal of Finance, 65*(5), 1915–1947.
Frino, A., & Gallaher, D. R. (2001). Tracking S&P500 index funds. *Journal of Portfolio Management, 28*(1), 44–55.
Froot, K. A., Scharfstein, D. S., & Stein, J. C. (1992). Herd on the street: Informational inefficiencies in a market with short-term speculation. *The Journal of Finance, 47*(4), 1461–1484.
Fuller, R. J. (1998). Behavioral finance and the sources of alpha. *Journal of Pension Plan Investing, 2*(3), 291–293.
Grinblatt, M., Titman, S., & Wemers, R. (1995). Momentum investment strategies, portfolio performance, and herding: A study of mutual fund behavior. *The American Economic Review, 85*(5), 1088–1105.
Grinold, R. C. (1989). The fundamental law of active management. *Streetwise: The Best of the Journal of Portfolio Management*, 161–168. https://books.google.it/books?hl=en&lr=&id=keA9DwAAQBAJ&oi=fnd&pg=PA161&dq=+grinold+law+active+management&ots=9jA3u4SKRB&sig=M0Weo52Ypy11-iUQpu3RvKVqUXA#v=onepage&q=grinold%20law%20active%20management&f=false.

Hirshleifer, D., Subrahmanyam, A., & Titman, S. (1994). Security analysis and trading patterns when some investors receive information before others. *The Journal of Finance, 49*(5), 1665–1698.

Jensen, M. C. (1968). The performance of mutual funds in the period 1945–1964. *The Journal of Finance, 23*(2), 389–416.

Lakonishok, J., Shleifer, A., & Vishny, R. W. (1992). The impact of institutional trading on stock prices. *Journal of Financial Economics, 32*(1), 23–43.

Malkiel, B. G. (1973). *A random walk down wall street*. Norton.

Massa, M., & Patgiri, R. (2008). Incentives and mutual fund performance: Higher performance or just higher risk taking? *Review of Financial Studies, 21*(1), 51–99.

Menkloff, L., Schmidt, E., & Brozynski, T. (2006). The impact of experience on risk raking, overconfidence, and herding of fund managers: Complementary survey evidence. *European Economic Review, 50*, 1753–1766.

Odean, T. (1999). Do investors trade too much? *American Economic Review, 89*, 1279–1298.

Pástor, L., & Stambaugh, R. F. (2012). On the size of the active management industry. *Journal of Political Economy, 120*(4), 740–781.

Scharfestein, D. S., & Stein J. C. (1990). Herd behavior and investment. *The American Economic Review, 80*(3), 465–479.

S&P Dow Jones Indices Research. (2021). SPIVA Scorecard report.

Sharma, V., Easterwood, J. C., & Kumar R. (2006). *Institutional herding and the internet bubble* (Working Paper Series).

Sharpe, W. (1991). Arithmetic of active management. *Financial Analysts Journal, 47*(1), 7–9.

Shefrin, H. (2000). *Beyond greed and fear*. Harvard University Press.

Shefrin, H., & Statman, M. (1985). The disposition to sell winners too early and ride losers too long: Theory and evidence. *The Journal of Finance, 40*, 777–790.

Siegel, L. B. (2003). *Benchmarks and investment management*. The Research Foundation of The Association for Investment Management and Research.

Trueman, B. (1988). A theory of noise trading in securities markets. *The Journal of Finance, 43*(1), 83–95.

CHAPTER 4

Searching for Market Drivers: Factor Investing

Abstract Factor investing is designed to select securities based on different market drivers among which, the first that have been identified from the academic literature are size, value, and momentum. Factor research has the objective of generating risk and return profiles that differ from traditional models, focusing on different market drivers compatible with investor expectations. This investment style can be considered somewhere between active management and passive management. Active because the research is that of active returns with respect to the market portfolio, passive because it is based on defined and transparent rules. In this chapter, we first focus on the origins of factors through the academic literature. Secondly, we move to the asset manager's perspective describing the various facets of factor investing in asset management. Finally, we focus on indexes aimed to describe each factor.

Keywords Factor investing · Smart beta · Fama and French three-factor model · Factor indexing

Factor investing is an investment approach that involves selecting stocks based on their exposure to specific factors or characteristics, rather than simply buying a diversified portfolio of stocks. Factors are persistent and pervasive drivers of return that have been identified in academic research.

E. Bolognesi, *New Trends in Asset Management*,
https://doi.org/10.1007/978-3-031-35057-3_4

The basic idea behind factor investing is to identify securities that exhibit strong exposure to a particular factor and to construct a portfolio that is overweight in those securities. In particular, factor investors use quantitative techniques to identify factors that are expected to generate excess returns, but do not rely on individual security selection or market timing to achieve these returns. Instead, they aim to capture the systematic and persistent returns associated with certain factors over time.

From the asset manager's perspective, factor investing is a sort of middle ground between passive and active management. On one hand, factor investing involves a systematic approach to portfolio construction that is based on a set of rules or criteria, rather than on the subjective opinions of portfolio managers. This approach is similar to passive management, where investments are made to track an index or benchmark, without the need for active decision-making. On the other hand, factor investing aims to generate excess returns by selecting securities that exhibit certain characteristics or factors. This approach is similar to active management, where portfolio managers aim to outperform the market by making active decisions on which securities to buy and sell.

The Theory Behind Factors

A factor is any characteristic that can explain the risk and return performance of an asset. Here it is worthwhile to recall the theory behind active portfolio management and then address those factors that are used in building up factor portfolios and indexes. As aforementioned, active portfolio managers have, for several decades, debated the efficiency market hypothesis. In this regard, the CAPM asserts that stock returns can be explained by just one factor, which is the market portfolio. However, market beta alone is not capable of explaining the overall return of a stock. Hence, academics claim that the CAPM is based on several unrealistic assumptions[1] that prevent it from being the ideal equilibrium model in

[1] Assumptions of the CAPM model: (*i*) all investors take a position on the efficient frontier where all investments are maximising utility and since investors are risk averse and utility maximising, they focus only on their return (mean) and the related risk (variance). The exact location on the efficient frontier which investors select for their portfolio will depend on their utility function and the trade-off between risk and return; (*ii*) investors can borrow or lend any funds at the risk-free rate of return; (*iii*) all investors have homogenous expectations, thus they make the same estimate regarding the expected

asset pricing. Considering these anomalies, Ross and Roll (1984) developed the Arbitrage Pricing Theory (APT), which is based on the idea that assets returns are not merely generated by one factor but, instead, by a set of factors able to capture broad risks across asset classes. Initially, these factors were sought among macroeconomic variables, such as gross domestic production (GDP), interest and exchange rates, oil prices, etc. Later, the focus shifted towards the so-called style factors, such as firms' size and other fundamental values. Two of the advantages of the APT model are that it does not need the strong assumptions of the CAPM and that it goes beyond the market portfolio concept. At the same time, however, the APT leaves open the problem of identifying the number and nature of relevant factors. Even if it is rather intuitive that the number of relevant factors should not be too high, the problem is the identification of the factors to be considered.

Certainly, the most famous multi-factor model is the one proposed by Eugene Fama and Kenneth French, published in the Journal of Financial Economics in 1993, based on three factors. In particular, this model focuses on the companies' size and on their book-to-market ratio as factors that can contribute to explaining stock returns. In particular, they built a three-factor model according to which the return of a single security or portfolio is explained by: *(i)* the reference market for the security/portfolio; *(ii)* the parameter *size* based on the stocks' market cap; *(iii)* the parameter *value*, based on the book-to-market ratio. To sum up, this model adds to the beta coefficient of the CAPM two new risk indicators based on the stocks' fundamentals. Empirically, the regression analysis is based on the following formula:

$$r_i - R_f = \alpha + \beta_{\text{mkt}_i} \cdot \left[R_{\text{mkt}} - R_f\right] + \beta_{\text{SMB}_i} \cdot \text{SMB} + \beta_{\text{HML}_i} \cdot \text{HML} + \varepsilon_i \tag{4.1}$$

where r_i is the portfolio return, R_{mkt} is the market return, R_f is the risk-free rate, SMB (Small Minus Big) is the difference between the returns of small caps and blue chips; HML (High Minus Low) is the difference in

return, variance and covariance of all investible risky assets; (*iv*) all investors hold investments for the same one-period of time; (*v*) investors are able to buy or sell portions from their shares of any security or a portfolio they hold; (*vi*) there are no taxes or transaction costs on purchasing or selling assets; (*vii*) there is no inflation or any change in interest rates; (*viii*) capital markets are in equilibrium, and all investments are fairly priced, consequently, investors can not affect prices.

returns of stocks with high and low book-to-market ratio; β_{mkt_i}, β_{SMB_i}, β_{HML_i} is the sensitivity of the portfolio to the reference market, size, and book-to-market factors.

The rationale behind this model is that larger companies are less risky than the smaller ones and, consequently, may offer lower expected returns. Conversely, the small caps generally present higher risk and, therefore, investors require a higher premium to compensate for the additional risk. The ratio between book-to-market values also holds a high explanatory power: high ratios (low Price-to-Book Value) characterise stocks with low expected growth and, therefore, less risky, and *vice versa*, securities that show a low ratio denote good growth opportunities and high intangible assets which are reflected in the market value rather than into the book value.

Following evolution of the Fama and French (FF) three-factor model is the four-factor model, introduced by Carhart in 1997, through a famous article published in the Journal of Finance. In this model, Carhart adds an additional factor called *momentum*. This factor is based on the results of Jegadeesh and Titman (1993) showing that the strategy of buying stocks that have performed well and selling stocks that have performed poorly generated significant positive returns over 3- to 12-month holding periods. Thus, momentum is the tendency of stocks that have outperformed to continue the outperformance in the future. Based on these results, a new variable, Winner Minus Losers, has been added to the model, computed as the difference between the returns of stocks with a positive performance (the winners) and stocks with a negative performance (the losers). Formally:

$$r_i - R_f = \alpha + \beta_{\mathrm{mkt}_i} \cdot \left[R_{\mathrm{mkt}} - R_f\right] + \beta_{\mathrm{SMB}_i} \cdot \mathrm{SMB} + \beta_{\mathrm{HML}_i} \cdot \mathrm{HML} + \beta_{\mathrm{WML}_i} \cdot \mathrm{WML} + \varepsilon_i \qquad (4.2)$$

More recently, in 2015, Fama and French adapted their model to include five factors. Along with the original three factors, the new model adds the concept that companies reporting higher future earnings show higher returns in the stock market, a factor referred to as *profitability*. In more detail, this factor is based on the operating profitability, 'OP', measured as the annual revenues minus the cost of goods sold, interest expense, selling, and general and administrative expenses during the previous fiscal year, divided by the end book value of equity. The construction of the OP-ranked benchmark portfolios permits the computation of the Robust minus Weak (RMW) factor. Furthermore, the fifth factor, referred to as *investment*, relates to the concept of internal investment and returns, suggesting that companies directing profit towards major growth projects are likely to experience losses in the stock market. The authors define the measure of asset growth, 'INV', as the change in the book value of total assets from the beginning to the end of the previous period, divided by the previous end book value of total assets. After the construction of the INV-ranked benchmark portfolios, they calculate the Conservative minus Aggressive (CMA) factor. Hence, the model is reshaped as follows:

$$
\begin{aligned}
r_i - R_f = \alpha + \beta_{\text{mkt}_i} \cdot \left[R_{\text{mkt}} - R_f\right] + \beta_{\text{SMB}_i} \cdot \text{SMB} + \beta_{\text{HML}_i} \cdot \text{HML} \\
+ \beta_{\text{RMW}_i} \cdot \text{RMW} + \beta_{\text{CMA}_i} \cdot \text{CMA} + \varepsilon_i \qquad (4.3)
\end{aligned}
$$

From the first FF three-factor model, multiple factors have been tested and academic research in this direction is constant. The impact of these factors in asset management has been significant as they represent what we now call management styles.

Fama–French Three-Factor Model: An Application to Alternative Weighting Schemes

An interesting implementation of the FF three-factor model is the analysis of the characteristics of the different index construction methodologies examined in Chapter 2. The statistics on portfolios' risk and return provided in Table 2.1 produces insights into how the indexes behave. However, it is also interesting to analyse where the return properties come from. The non-cap-weighted indexes may take on exposures to the additional risk factors, i.e., value and small-cap exposure. Following the FF model (Eq. 4.1) the first step is to select suitable indexes to construct the explanatory variables. Focusing on the US equity market, the analysis is based on weekly returns of the following indexes: S&P 500 Index as the market portfolio; S&P 100 Index as a basket of blue chip stocks; S&P 400 Mid Cap Index as a basket of mid-caps (the bottom 400 of the S&P 500 Index); S&P 500 Value Index as a basket of high book-to-market stocks; and S&P 500 Growth Index as a basket of low book-to-market stocks. The observation period is 2003–2023.

Table 4.1 reports the results. The *Alpha* coefficients are not significant, except in case of the Efficiency Index, suggesting an outperformance, not explained by the explanatory factors, equal to 2.70% on a yearly basis. Moreover, the beta coefficients (calculated against the S&P 500 Index) are qualitatively similar to what was obtained in Table 2.1: our findings confirm the low beta nature of the minimum volatility index (0.80), whereas the other indexes present betas reasonably close to 1. Overall, SMB beta coefficients, when statistically significant, are positive. Similarly, the value/growth exposure indicates that the index components' compositions tilt towards value stocks if compared to the S&P 500 index. In fact, each of the HML beta coefficients is negative and statistically significant. These findings can appear counterintuitive in some cases and must be examined in more depth.

As expected, the *fundamental-weighted index* shows the lowest HML beta coefficient (−0.40) confirming that it is aimed at rewarding companies showing the best fundamentals. Thus, stocks characterised by higher earnings yields are mechanically overweighted, whereas stocks with a low earnings yield are underweighted. Similar evidence can be identified concerning the firms' characteristics selected by the index method, notably dividends, book value, and sales. Stocks with a high dividend yield, high book-to-market ratio, and high sales-to-price ratio should be overweighted compared with their capitalisation weight. As these are typical ratios used in value strategies, it is not surprising to find a substantial exposure to the value factor. Moreover, the SMB beta coefficient is

Table 4.1 Comparison between alternative weighting schemes

	Fundamental weighted	*Equal weighted*	*Efficient weighted*	*Min volatility weighted*
Alpha (Ann)	1.28	1.02	2.70**	2.43
Market exposure	1.02***	1.05***	0.98***	0.82***
HML	(0.40)***	(0.21)***	(0.13)***	(0.13)***
SMB	0.09***	0.23***	0.20***	(0.05)**
R^2	0.98	0.98	0.98	0.90

Analyses are based on weekly returns. *Source* Bloomberg Data. Author computation
***, **, * Indicate statistical significance at the 1 percent, 5 percent, and 10 percent levels, respectively

positive (0.12) meaning that the fundamental index presents a higher weight on small caps compared to the cap weighted.

Also, in the case of the *equal-weighted index* we find a positive SMB beta (0.34) and a negative HML beta coefficient (−0.20). This latter result is quite surprising because the construction methodology is neutral and should be free of any value or growth bias. In fact, since no information whatsoever on valuation influences the determination of its weights, it is difficult to imagine that such an index would imply any choices in terms of value or growth exposure. Thus, if we revert the analysis and consider the equal-weighted index as a reference for value/growth neutrality, the direct implication is that the bias is to be attributed to the cap-weighted index. This evidence allows the argument that the cap-weighted index presents a growth bias relative to the equal-weighted index. Focusing on the SMB beta coefficient, it is not surprising that its positive sign and its value are the highest of the indexes group. This methodology imposes equal weights for which the mid-caps have the same weight as the blue chips. It is therefore natural to expect that the coefficient is the highest among indexes.

The *efficient-weighted index* is the only one presenting a statistically significant alpha coefficient (2.26). This result confirms our previous findings (see Table 2.1): the efficient-weighted index shows the highest shape ratio of the group. The SMB beta coefficient is high and equal to 0.33 suggesting higher weights of mid-caps when compared with the S&P 500 Index. The HML beta coefficient is (−0.11) confirming the previously mentioned evidence that the cap-weighted index presents a bias towards value stocks.

Finally, the *minimum volatility index* does not present a statistically significant SMB beta coefficient, meaning that the portfolio concentration in low beta stocks does not lead to any bias related to the stocks' size. Finally, also in this case the HML beta coefficient is negative, presenting the same value of the efficient-weighted index (−0.11): this evidence suggests that the two indexes are less exposed to the value bias.

Smart Beta and Factor Investing

The outlined academic results on the impact of different factors on indexes returns have progressively declined in the asset management industry with the launch of investment products based on strategies firstly aimed at deviating from the traditional cap-weighting approach. As a consequence, the term *Smart beta* has gained popularity and gathers all alternative forms of indexations departing from cap-weighting, that aims to generate superior risk-adjusted returns, compared to traditional indexation.

Smart beta was initially conceived as a response to two already mentioned drawbacks of market-cap indexes. As summarised by Amenc et al. (2011), the first drawback is that such portfolios typically provide limited access to long-term rewarded risk factors such as size or value, among others. The second problem with cap-weighting is the lack of efficient diversification to the systematic risks due to excessive concentration in the largest cap stocks. Some examples of Smart beta strategies are, among others, the following: low volatility, value, fundamentally weighted, high quality, momentum, risk parity, dividend yield, maximum diversification, minimum variance, and equal weight. The primary objectives for the use of Smart beta are risk reduction, return enhancement, and improving diversification. Smart beta strategies are now widely available in ETFs and mutual funds, making factor strategies affordable and accessible to every investor.

Similarly, *Factor investing* is an investment approach that involves targeting specific drivers of return across asset classes. In other words, it is an investment paradigm under which an investor decides how much to allocate to various factors, as opposed to various securities or asset classes. Its popularity has been growing since the turn of the millennium, especially after the recognition in 2008 that multiple asset classes can experience severe losses at the same time despite their apparent differences (Martellini & Milhau, 2018).

As already mentioned, in the view of many academics, factor investing lies between active and passive management. If we consider it from the active point of view, this strategy helps managers to generate active returns, thus creating alpha. If we turn to the passive management perspective, factor investing is presented as rule-based and transparency implementation. Thus, factor investing still tries to follow the EMH presented by the Eugene Fama, but it is also based on the search for long-term drivers of performance. Figure 4.1 provides a representation of this idea.

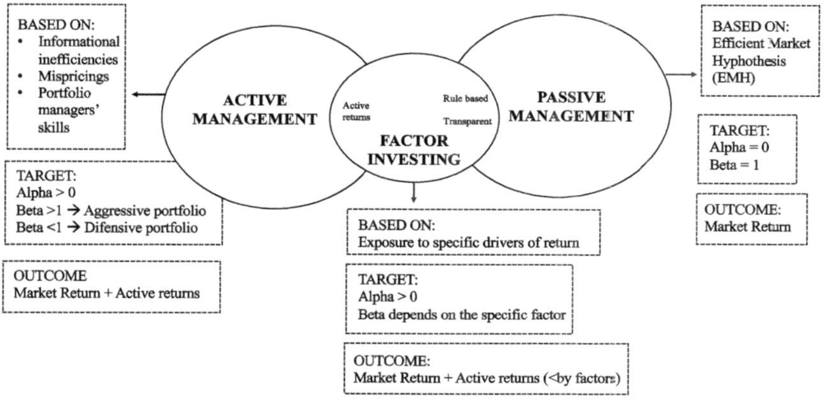

Fig. 4.1 Factor investing as a middle ground between active and passive investing (*Source* Author's elaboration)

Factor Investing and the Asset Management Industry

Many institutional investors have approached factor investing over years. The importance of factors in describing the investment strategies followed by equity portfolios is quite tangible if we think of the famous Style Box proposed for the first time in 1992 by Morningstar, a leading provider of investment research and analysis. The *Morningstar Style Box* is illustrated in Fig. 4.2: it is a simple 9-square grid that is used to classify mutual funds based on two factors: size (market capitalisation) and value/growth orientation. Each mutual fund is assigned a placement within the Style Box based on its underlying holdings. For example, a mutual fund that primarily invests in large-cap value stocks would be placed in the bottom-left square of the Style Box. Its simplicity has been appreciated to such an extent that the Style Box has become a fund categorisation standard used by investors to quickly understand the investment style and compare mutual funds.

Progressively, the world's leading asset managers have devised factor-based products in offering both mutual funds and ETFs. Among these, we mention: BlackRock, Vanguard, State Street Global Advisors, Invesco, Northern Trust Asset Management, JPMorgan Asset Management, and Goldman Sachs Asset Management.

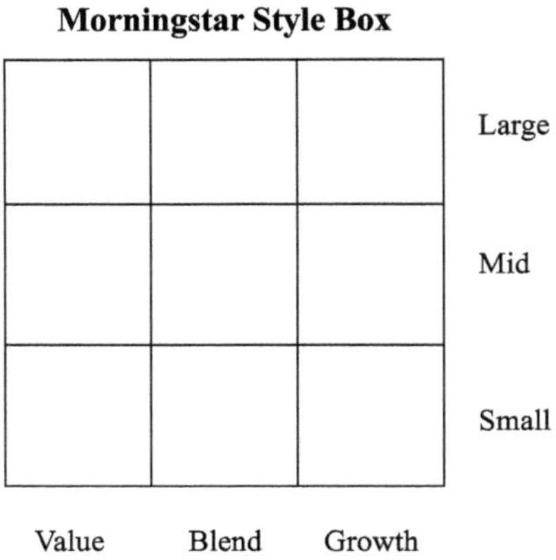

Fig. 4.2 The Morningstar's style box investing (*Source* Morningstar website)

Focusing on BlackRock, one of the leaders in factor investing, the launch of the first-factor fund dates back to 1971. The idea behind this choice is that factors are broad and persistent drivers of return that are critical to helping investors who are seeking a range of goals from generating returns and reducing risk to improving diversification. It is also interesting how they communicate factor investing to potential investors, defining factors as the foundation of investing: 'Just as *nutrients* are the foundations of the food we eat. Similarly, knowing the factors that drive returns in your portfolio can help you to choose the right mix of assets and strategies for your needs'. Moreover, the asset manager identifies two main types of factors that drive returns. On the one hand, macro factors, like the pace of economic growth and the rate of inflation can help to explain returns across asset classes like equity or bond markets. On the other hand, style factors can help explain returns within those asset classes. Factors can help us build portfolios that better suit individual needs; just as knowing the nutrients in your food can help your body perform. Similarly, investors looking for downside protection in a volatile market environment might add exposure to minimum volatility strategies to seek reduced risk, while investors who are comfortable accepting increased risk might look to more return-seeking strategies like momentum.

Vanguard defines factor-based funds as a form of actively managed funds. They purposely *tilt portfolios* towards certain stock characteristics, like recent momentum, higher quality, or lower stock prices to achieve specific risk and return objectives. The asset manager argues that factor funds may be appropriate for the experienced long-term investor who wants to pursue specific factors but is looking for more transparency with respect to in a traditional actively managed fund. Moreover, this kind of investment is not expected to serve as a core investment, but a tool to tilt a portion of the portfolio in an attempt to augment its performance.

Factor timing is extremely difficult, and strategies that attempt to do so are ill-advised. So be sure you have the long-term patience needed to stick with a factor-based investment strategy.

Finally, we rely on Invesco AM that believes that factor investing has the potential to drive more precise investment and asset allocation decisions in an attempt to optimise a truly diversified portfolio targeting a specific risk/return objective. Moreover, the asset manager argues that a factor-based investment approach seeks exposure to particular factors rather than focusing on sectors, geographies, or investment styles.

Factor Indexing

The implementation and diffusion of this investment strategy has been supported by the creation of *factor indexes* to be used as benchmarks. For example, Morgan Stanley Global Investment (MSCI) Solutions, a lead index provider, has been offering indexes based on multiple factors since 2018. It is interesting to explore the factors selected by MSCI for the construction of the related indexes, which are a selection based both on evidence from academic research and on empirical evidence and deriving from back-testing activities. The first set of factors provided has been focused on volatility, dividend yield, quality, momentum, growth and value bias, and firms' size.

Starting from the most popular factors, the preference towards the *size* factor, which translates into investment in medium–small sized securities, is based on empirical evidence demonstrating the persistence of the outperformance obtained, over the long term, by small-cap stocks. Size is categorised as a 'pro-cyclical' factor, meaning that it has tended to benefit during periods of economic expansion. The size premium has been evidenced by Fama and French (Eq. 4.1) and has been part of institutional investing for decades. In the past few years, it has become a building block of many factor-based indexes. On this issue, Banz (1981) examined the relationship between the size of a company and its stock returns using data from the New York Stock Exchange for the period 1936–1975. He found evidence of a positive relationship between a company's market value (i.e., its size) and its average return, but this relationship was weaker for the smallest and largest companies. This evidence established the size effect as a significant empirical regularity in finance. He argued that the size effect could not be explained by traditional asset pricing models, such as the Capital Asset Pricing Model (CAPM), which assumes that higher returns are associated with higher risk. MSCI has associated this factor with the MSCI Equal-Weighted Indexes because it tends to overweight smaller cap companies relative to the benchmark parent index. Index components are weighted equally at each rebalance date, effectively removing the influence of that constituent's price (high or low) from the index.

The additional factor discovered by Fama and French supports the *value* investing meaning that, over the long term, undervalued stocks outperform more expensive stocks. Piotroski (2000) confirms this idea, showing that companies with improving financial performance, as measured by a combination of profitability, liquidity, and other fundamental factors, present higher returns than companies with deteriorating financial performance. Value is captured through different market multiples such as book-to-price and earnings yield. The foundation of value investing is the notion that cheaply priced stocks outperform pricier stocks in the long term. Value is categorised as a 'pro-cyclical' factor, meaning it has tended to benefit during periods of economic expansion. Value has several dimensions. For example, MSCI Enhanced Value Index applies three valuation ratio descriptors on a sector relative basis: Forward price to earnings (Fwd P/E); Enterprise value/operating cash flows (EV/CFO), and Price-to-Book value (P/B). MSCI claims that the index aims to address the pitfalls of value investing, among them 'value traps meaning stocks that appear cheap but which in fact do not appreciate'. Their analysis shows that using forward earnings has helped provide protection against value traps, and that whole firm valuation measures, such as enterprise value, have reduced concentration in highly leveraged companies, meaning those that have borrowed heavily. Many investors use this approach in identifying assets that they expect the market to revalue. It is worth mentioning that indices built according to the value style use the same investment philosophy as indices built according to fundamental indexation.

Following the results of Jegadeesh and Titman (1993) and the four-factor model of Charart (see Eq. 4.2), the *momentum* factor refers to the tendency of winning stocks to continue performing well in the near term. In other words, it takes advantage of market trends and focuses on stocks that have outperformed the market because they have greater relative strength. Many studies since then have found the momentum factor present across equity sectors, countries, and more broadly asset classes. MSCI categorises the momentum factor as a 'persistence' factor, i.e., it tends to benefit from continued trends in markets. The index provider highlights that momentum is not well understood as other factors, although various theories attempt to explain it. Some postulate that it is compensation for bearing high risk; others believe it may be a consequence of market inefficiencies produced by delayed price reactions to firm-specific information.

The ***minimum volatility*** is a strategy that involves buying stocks based on the estimate of their volatility and correlations with other stocks. Minimum volatility is categorised as a 'defensive' factor, meaning that it has tended to benefit during periods of economic contraction. As discussed by MSCI, the key objective of this strategy is to capture regional and global exposure to stocks with potentially less risk. Tactical investors have used MSCI Minimum Volatility Indexes to reduce risk during market downturns, while retaining exposure to equity. The minimum volatility premium (MVP) refers to the excess returns that can be earned by investing in low-volatility stocks. The idea is that stocks with lower volatility should, on average, provide higher risk-adjusted returns than more volatile stocks. The MVP is the minimum level of this excess return that investors should expect to receive. One theory posits that investors underpay for low-volatility stocks, viewing them as less rewarding, and overpay for high-volatility stocks that are seen as long-shot opportunities for higher returns. Moreover, investors can be overconfident in their ability to forecast the future, and their opinions can differ more for high-volatility stocks, which have less certain outcomes, leading to higher volatility and lower returns. In terms of methodology, the main approaches to implementing a minimum volatility strategy fall into two groups: (1) simple rank and selection and (2) optimisation-based solutions. A simple approach ranks the universe of stocks by their expected volatility, selects a subset of the constituents from the universe, and then applies a weighting method. These approaches generally ignore the correlation between stock returns, which can have a significant impact on the overall volatility strategy. While a simple rank and selection method reflects the volatility of individual stocks, optimisation-based approaches account for both volatility and correlation effects, i.e., the magnitude and the degree to which stocks move in tandem. However, a naive unconstrained minimum volatility strategy has its own set of challenges, such as biases towards certain sectors and countries, unwanted factor exposures, and potentially high turnover at rebalancing. Well-designed optimisations with carefully constructed constraints, however, may be able to neutralise these shortcomings.

Another example of defensive strategy is the *high dividend yield* strategy which gains exposure to companies that appear undervalued and have demonstrated stable and increasing dividends. Index constituents of the MSCI High Dividend Yield Indexes are selected not only on the basis of the dividend yield, generally at least 30% higher than the average dividend yield of the market, but also on fundamentals. Investors may focus on the equity dividend income because they are seeking income outside of the fixed income. Several theories seek to explain the superior performance of high dividend stocks. One notes that yield investors have preferred dividend payouts in the present to uncertain capital gains in the future. They have also tended to view dividend increases as a sign of future profitability. Several studies show that dividend yields have been strong indicators of earnings growth. Fama and French (1988) show that high dividend yields are associated with high expected returns and that the dividend yield is a strong predictor of future earnings growth. Arnott and Asness (2003) analysed data from 1972 to 2001 and found that companies that increase their dividends tend to have higher earnings growth in subsequent years. Moreover, Shiller (1981) and Campbell and Shiller (1988) showed that dividends are a good indicator of future earnings growth and that companies that pay high dividends tended to have more stable earnings.

The *quality* factor is also a defensive factor because based on the fundamentals of companies, rewarding those with durable business models and sustainable competitive advantages. For example, some measures used in stock selection are return on equity (or ROE), leverage, and earnings variability. This factor is based on Fama and French five-factor model (see Eq. 4.3) presenting a relationship between stock returns and fundamentals. From an operational point of view, the MSCI Quality Index employs three fundamental variables to capture the quality factor: Return on equity (which shows how effectively a company uses investments to generate earnings growth); Debt to equity (a measure of company leverage); and Earnings variability (how smooth earnings growth has been). Furthermore, MSCI argues that many active strategies have emphasised quality growth as an important factor in their security selection and portfolio construction. Focusing on academic literature, Novy-Marx (2012) examines the relationship between company profitability and stock returns. He shows that companies with high gross profitability (defined as gross profits to total assets) present higher returns than companies with low gross profitability, even after controlling for traditional value and size factors. He argues that gross profitability is a better measure of a company's economic profitability than earnings-based measures, such as return on equity (ROE) or earnings before interest and taxes (EBIT). This is because earnings-based measures can be affected by accounting decisions, while gross profitability is based on a company's ability to generate revenue after accounting for the costs of goods sold. Fama and French (2015) show that profitability is one of five key factors that explained differences in stock returns. They defined profitability as operating income before depreciation and amortisation scaled by book equity.

Finally, the attention towards factor investing is evidenced by the growth both of assets under management towards specialised products in this segment, and by the study of new factors, such as *liquidity*, based on trading and turnover statistics of selected securities and *growth*, based on the revenue and profit growth. Finally, the evolution of factor investing is certainly a multi-factor investment allowing additional benefit from diversification in investing on different factors.

To better understand the characteristics of these most popular factors, we proceed with the analysis of the corresponding MSCI Indexes. In order to exclude geographical and currency implications of the portfolios' composition, we focus on the US equity market. The indexes selected are listed in Table 4.2. The cap-weighted portfolio is associated with the MSCI US Index.

Factor Investing: A Back-Test Exercise

We analyse the risk-return profile of factor indexes over a 20-year period, from 2003 to 2023. We rely on the MSCI Indexes described in Table 4.2. We calculate returns and standard deviations on a weekly frequency using Bloomberg. Results, on a yearly basis, are presented in Fig. 4.3. Looking at the statistics of returns, it is important to underline that results can change considerably depending on the time window considered. In this analysis, the choice has been to extend the observation period as much as possible, depending on the data availability.

Table 4.2 Factors and indexes description

Factor	*MCSI index*	*Description*
Quality	MCSI quality index	The Quality factor is aimed at capturing companies with durable business models and sustainable competitive advantages
Yield	MCSI high dividend yield index	A yield investment strategy gains exposure to companies that appear undervalued and have demonstrated stable and increasing dividends
Growth	MCSI growth index	The Growth factor captures company growth prospects using historical earnings, sales and predicted earnings
Value	MCSI value index	Value investing is premised on identifying stocks whose prices seem to understand their intrinsic value
Volatility	MCSI minimum volatility index	A minimum volatility strategy involves buying stocks based on the estimate of their volatility and correlations with other stocks
Momentum	MCSI momentum index	The Momentum factor refers to the tendency of winning stocks to continue performing well in the near term
Size	MCSI equal weight index	The Size factor capture the tendency of small-cap stocks to outperform bigger companies over the long run

Source Author elaboration on MSCI data

Observing the chart, it is possible to draw the following considerations: *(i)* Dominant portfolios, according to the mean–variance principle, are the minimum volatility, the quality, and the momentum, whereas the latter presents the highest risk. *(ii)* As expected, the most conservative portfolio is minimum volatility, followed by quality and dividend yield. *(iii)* The portfolio presenting the highest volatility is the small cap, but its high level of risk is not rewarded by a high return if compared to other portfolios. *(iv)* The worst portfolio, in terms of risk-return profile is the value. Here it is interesting to note the remarkable difference between the value and the quality portfolios because, ideally, they could be considered quite similar. On the contrary, in this analysis, they show opposite characteristics: in fact, the quality portfolio is dominant while the value is dominated by all other portfolios. *(v)* Generally, growth and value styles are considered to be opposites but, in this analysis, they present fairly similar levels of risk. *(vi)* The cap-weighted portfolio is positioned in the middle of all other portfolios in terms of both risk and return. Therefore,

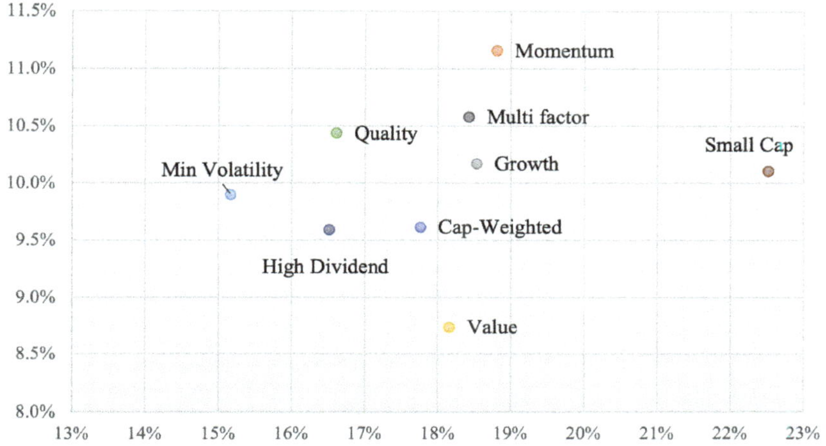

Fig. 4.3 Factor indexes: Risk-return profile (Analyses are based on weekly returns. Observing period: January 2003–January 2023. *Source* Bloomberg Data. Author computation)

assuming that each portfolio is mainly composed of the same stocks (at least, US stocks), but in different proportions, the cap-weighted portfolio becomes a sort of point of reference, and that each strategy moves away from it in a different measure and direction. *(vii)* The multifactor represents a synthesis of all the styles. It presents a risk profile similar to that of the cap weighted but a significantly higher return.

To sum up, factor investing is designed to select securities based on different market drivers and aims at achieving the following goals:

1. *Improved Risk-Adjusted Returns*: Factor investing aims to identify securities that have higher expected returns than the overall market, while also managing risk. By focusing on factors that are associated with higher returns, factor investing can potentially provide better risk-adjusted returns than traditional market cap-weighted approaches.
2. *Diversification*: Factor investing can provide diversification benefits by investing in securities that are not necessarily correlated with each other. By combining different factors, investors can potentially reduce overall portfolio risk.

3. *Transparency*: Factor investing typically involves a rules-based approach, where securities are selected based on certain predefined criteria. This can provide greater transparency than traditional active management approaches, where investment decisions may be based on subjective criteria.
4. *Lower Costs*: Factor investing can potentially be less expensive than traditional active management approaches, as it typically involves passive or semi-passive investment strategies that are implemented through index funds or ETFs.
5. *Flexibility*: Factor investing can be tailored to individual investors' needs and preferences. Investors can choose to invest in factors that are aligned with their investment goals, risk tolerance, and other factors.

References

Amenc, N., Goltz, F., Martellini, L., & Ye, S. (2011). *Improved beta? A comparison of index-weighting schemes*. EDHEC-Risk Institute.

Arnott, R. D., & Asness, C. S. (2003). Surprise! Higher dividends = higher earnings growth. *Financial Analysts Journal, 59*(1), 70–87.

Banz, R. W. (1981). The relationship between return and market value of common stocks. *Journal of Financial Economics, 9*(1), 3–19.

Campbell, J. Y., & Shiller, R. J. (1988). Stock prices, earnings, and expected dividends. *The Journal of Finance, 43*(3), 661–676.

Fama, E. F., & French, K. R. (1988). Dividend yields and expected stock returns. *Journal of Financial Economics, 22*(1), 3–25. ISSN 0304-405X, https://www.sciencedirect.com/science/article/abs/pii/0304405X88900207.

Fama, E. F., & French, K. R. (2015). A five-factor asset pricing model. *Journal of Financial Economics, 116*(1), 1–22.

Jagadeesh, N., & Titman, S. (1993). Returns to buying winners and selling losers: Implications for stock market efficiency. *The Journal of Finance, XLVIII*(1), 65–91.

Martellini, L., & Milhau. V. (2018). *Smart beta and beyond: Maximising the benefits of factor investing*. EDHEC-Risk Institute Publication.

Novy-Marx, R. (2012). Is momentum really momentum? *Journal of Financial Economics, 103*(3), 429–453.

Piotroski, J. D. (2000). Value investing: The use of historical financial statement information to separate winners from losers. *Journal of Accounting Research*, 1–41.

Roll, R., & Ross, S. A. (1984). The arbitrage pricing theory approach to strategic portfolio planning. *Financial Analysts Journal, 40*(3), 14–26.
Shiller, R. J. (1981). Do stock prices move too much to be justified by subsequent changes in dividends? *American Economic Review, 71*, 421–436.

CHAPTER 5

Hybrids Increasingly Blurring Active/Passive Line

Abstract This chapter focuses on the exponential growth of passive management and on the evolution of this industry. We first focus on the birth of Index Funds and Exchange-Traded Funds, providing several statistics on the dynamics of passive investing in the equity markets. Therefore, we focus on the main developments of this sector and the advance of hybrids that are erasing what was once a clear line between active and passive management. As a consequence, active and passive investment products are moving closer and closer, so much so that they have begun to overlap: examples are Smart beta ETFs and Active ETFs.

Keywords Index funds · ETFs · Smart beta · Active ETFs · Active Non-Transparent ETFs

As discussed in Chapter 4, active management is suffering several threats, among which the most important from the investors' perspective is the overall underperformance of active funds. As already mentioned, this result is supported by the Efficient Market Hypothesis (EMH) suggesting that financial markets are 'informationally efficient', meaning that all available information about a security is already reflected in its current price. According to EMH, it is impossible to consistently beat the market through active management because all available information is already

E. Bolognesi, *New Trends in Asset Management*,
https://doi.org/10.1007/978-3-031-35057-3_5

incorporated into the price, and any attempt to outperform the market is based on luck rather than skill. The consequence is the difficulty for active managers to consistently outperform the market, making passive management a more attractive option for investors who believe in EMH. By investing in a passive fund that tracks a market index, investors achieve similar returns as the market pays lower fees than active funds.

In and around the 1960s, a confluence of factors (in particular the advent of computers) allowed a small group of academics to verify how money managers were performing versus the US stock market. One of their findings was famously articulated by Burton Malkiel in his 1973 book, *A Random Walk Down Wall Street*, in which he argued that 'a blindfolded monkey throwing darts at the stock listings' would do as well as the pros. The author argues that stock prices are largely random and unpredictable in the short term, and therefore, attempts to consistently beat the market through active management are unlikely to succeed. This means that trying to beat the market by identifying undervalued stocks or predicting market trends is a fruitless effort, and that investors are better off adopting a passive investment strategy, such as investing in index funds or ETFs, that aims to match the performance of the overall market or a particular market index (Malkiel, 2003, 2005). He also argues that investors should focus on asset allocation and diversification rather than stock picking, as spreading investments across different asset classes and sectors can reduce risk and potentially improve long-term returns. Furthermore, Malkiel emphasises the importance of keeping investment costs low and avoiding market timing and other forms of speculation that can lead to poor investment outcomes.

It is on these assumptions that the role of the market portfolio assumes central importance in asset management and, therefore, the observation and attention paid to market indices.

Index Portfolios and Exchange-Traded Funds

The search for market performance, as a more efficient and economical management strategy compared to the active one, has led to the creation of funds specialising in replicating the composition of the benchmarks. Therefore, index funds have inevitably become popular in financial market, although they did not receive the full attention from investors in the beginning. In fact, index funds had been around since the 1970s, they were initially only available to institutional investors and had high minimum investment requirements. The first retail index fund was launched by Vanguard Group on 31 August 1976. The fund was called the Vanguard 500 Index Fund and it tracked the performance of the S&P 500 Index, allowing individual investors to invest in a diversified portfolio of stocks with low fees. This index fund has been a major milestone in the development of passive investing and index funds, and it has since become one of the largest and most popular index funds in the world.

The transition from Index Funds to Exchange-Traded Funds (ETFs) occurred gradually over several years, starting in the 1990s. Like index funds, ETFs seek to replicate the performance of a particular index, but it is traded like an individual stock on an exchange. Thus, the main difference between index funds and ETFs is their greater flexibility: ETFs can be traded throughout the day, allowing investors to buy and sell shares at any time, while index funds can only be bought or sold at the end of the trading day. ETFs also have lower expense ratios than most index funds, making them an attractive option for investors looking to minimise costs.

The first ETF, known as the Toronto Index Participation Shares (TIPS), was introduced on the Toronto Stock Exchange in 1990 with the aim of tracking the Toronto 35 Index. However, the TIPS ETF was short-lived and only traded for a few months before being delisted. The first ETF to gain widespread popularity and become a major force in the financial industry was the SPDR S&P 500 ETF, which was launched in the United States in 1993 by State Street Global Advisors. Its nickname 'Spider' is derived from the fund's ticker symbol, which is 'SPY'.

Since then, the growth of passive management has been steady. In order to better understand this phenomenon, especially in the equity sector, it is useful to compare the evolution of Asset under Management (AuM) between active funds and passively managed funds (index funds + ETFs). Figure 5.1 shows the success of AuM under passive management compared to those funds under active management, by late 2019. At the end of 2022, passively managed funds exceeded actively managed funds by more than 1.5 trillion. It should also be noted that in the entire observation period, the passively managed funds are approximately half index funds and half ETFs.

Focusing in more depth on the ETFs industry, the multiplication of ETFs occurred rapidly, first by offering the replication of all the main world market indexes. Subsequently, the industry expanded towards the replication of management strategies typical of active management. The following statistics are aimed at tracing the evolution of this industry over

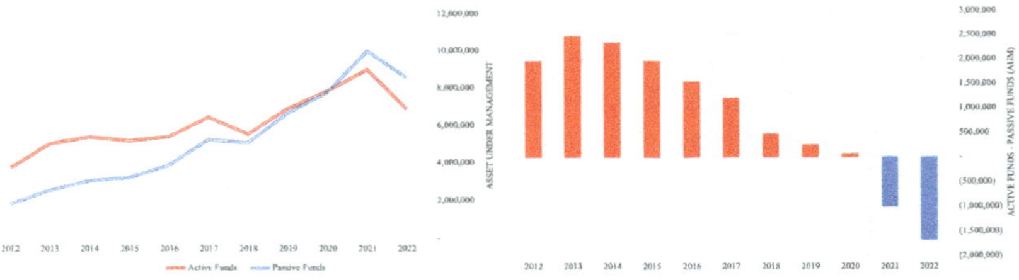

Fig. 5.1 Active vs passive equity funds: AuM (*Source* Author's elaboration on Bloomberg data)

time. Focusing on the dynamic of the AuM, Fig. 5.2 shows the huge growth of this industry. By late 2022, the total amount of AuM in ETFs was nearly 6.5 trillion USD and mainly focused on the equity market.

The geographic focus of equity ETFs is mainly on the US stock market. Figure 5.3 clearly shows this evidence and denotes the strong contribution of the US asset managers in the evolution of this investment tool.

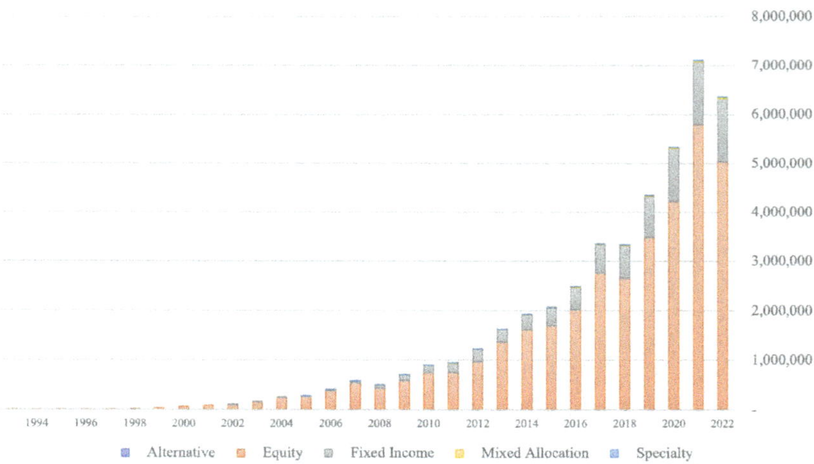

Fig. 5.2 ETFs industry: AuM (*Source* Author's elaboration on Bloomberg data)

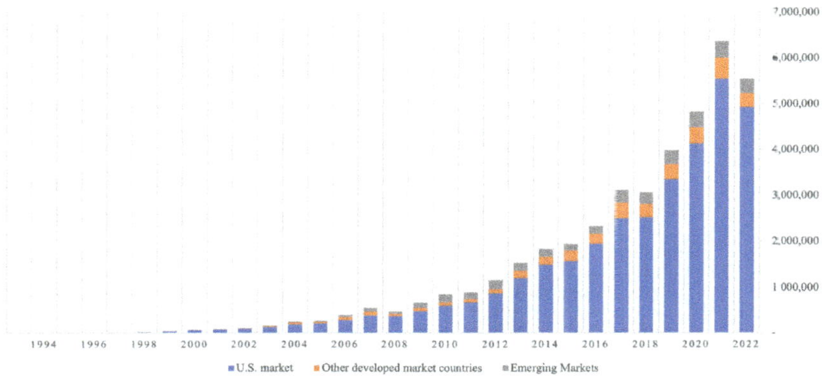

Fig. 5.3 Geographical focus of ETFs: AuM (*Source* Author's elaboration on Bloomberg data)

Other interesting statistics on the ETFs dynamic are related to the stock's size in the portfolios. As can be seen in Fig. 5.4, at the beginning (1993) the focus was only on the main US index, which implied investment exclusively in large caps. In 1995, the first funds specialised in mid-caps were launched, while the interest in small caps dates back to 2000. By the end of 2022, small caps represent nearly 10% of the equity market.

The Active–Passive Investment Line

If a decade ago the definitions of active and passive management were clearly distinct, over time the line has progressively blurred. At the beginning of the 2000s, the two sectors had clear objectives and the opposition was between the search for active returns (alpha), through the leverage of beta or stock picking skills, or the return of the market.

Gradually the two management philosophies have progressively converged. Starting with active management, risk management constraints have increasingly tied managers to benchmarks, making active management subject almost exclusively to relative return versus the market rather than absolute return oriented. Due to these constraints, active managements have progressively moved closer to the so-called semi-active managements. On the other hand, thanks to the success of

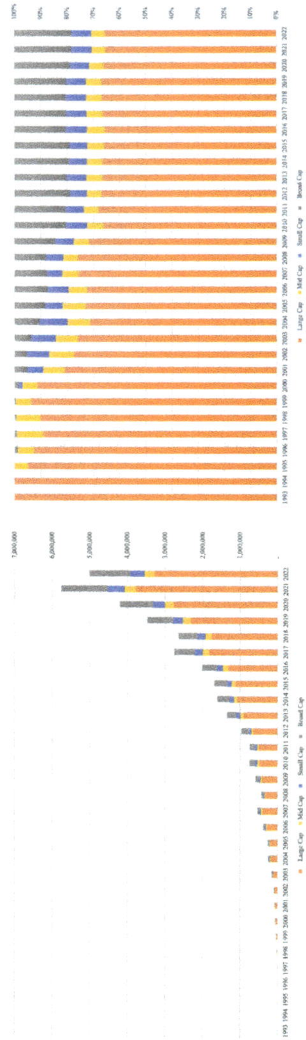

Fig. 5.4 Size focus of ETFs: AuM and percentage (*Source* Author's elaboration on Bloomberg data)

ETFs and the progress made by index providers in the creation of new market indexes, passive management has progressively moved towards the typical strategies of active management, such as those based on sectors. This evolution of ETFs has been rapid and has had the effect of increasing pressure on active funds.

Core-Satellite Strategy

A sort of compromise between active and passive management is semi-active management. By following this strategy, the manager seeks to achieve a return slightly higher than that of the benchmark by deciding on some cautious and controlled deviations. Operationally, the most popular approach is the *core-satellite strategy*.

As illustrated in Fig. 5.5, this strategy involves dividing the portfolio into two parts: a 'core' part and a 'satellite' part. The core part of the portfolio is typically invested in low cost, passively managed funds, such as index funds or ETFs, that aim to track the broad market. The core portion of the portfolio is designed to provide a stable, diversified foundation of investments that capture the overall performance of the market. The satellite part of the portfolio is invested in actively managed funds that target specific investment strategies. The satellite part of the portfolio is designed to provide an opportunity for alpha generation by taking advantage of the inefficiencies in the market.

The overall goal of the core-satellite strategy is to achieve a balance between cost-effective passive investing and active investing that seeks

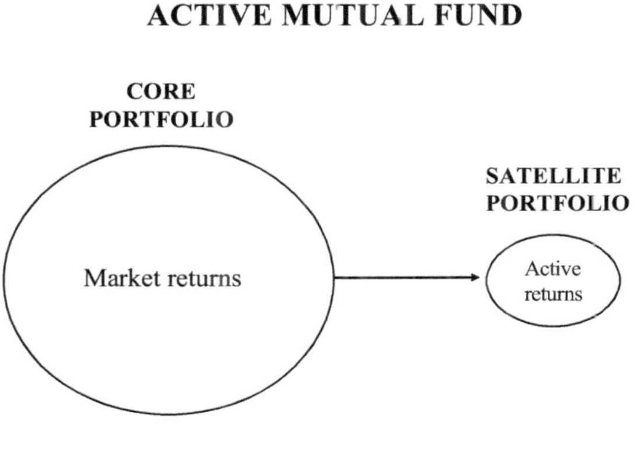

Fig. 5.5 Core-satellite strategy (*Source* Author's elaboration)

to outperform the market. By using a combination of passive and active investment strategies, the core-satellite approach aims to achieve the benefits of both approaches, namely low-cost diversification and the potential for alpha generation through active management.

Smart Beta ETFs

Smart beta ETFs are funds that follow rules-based investment strategies that seek to capture specific factors or characteristics that are believed to drive returns. As already mentioned in this chapter, a Smart beta approach is based on factors such as size, value, momentum, high dividend yield, etc. The purpose is to construct a portfolio of securities that are designed to outperform the traditional market capitalisation-weighted indices.

Smart beta ETFs aim to provide investors with a better risk-return profile than traditional passive ETFs while maintaining the benefits of low cost and diversification. Smart beta investing combines the benefits of passive investing and the advantages of active investing strategies. The goal of Smart beta is to obtain alpha, lower risk, or increase diversification at a cost lower than traditional active management and marginally higher than straight index investing.

Figure 5.6, graph (a), presents the dynamics of the industry of Smart beta ETFs in terms of AuM. The graphs also show the amount invested in the specific factors. By the end of 2022, the AuM was nearly 1.3 trillion USD. Graph (b) highlights more clearly the dynamic of the different factors. It is interesting to notice that until 2002 the industry has mainly focused on investment strategies of value and growth. Subsequently, size and dividend yield have been introduced. Finally, since 2011 an increasingly significant share of AuM has been positioned on products focused on minimising volatility.

For a better understanding of the popularity of this investment tool, it is interesting to dwell on another comparison, in particular between Smart beta and sectoral ETFs. Even the latter, introduced in the early 2000s, aimed to move away from portfolios based on geographical allocation in order to take advantage of different phases of the economic cycle. For example, in phases of economic expansion, cyclical sectors are favoured while in phases of slowdown, consumer staples, and healthcare are preferred. Moreover, sectorial ETFs track, like traditional ETFs, cap-weighted indexes. However, they are used for tactical portfolio allocation. Figure 5.7 show the dynamics of the AuM: as can be seen, if in 2012 the

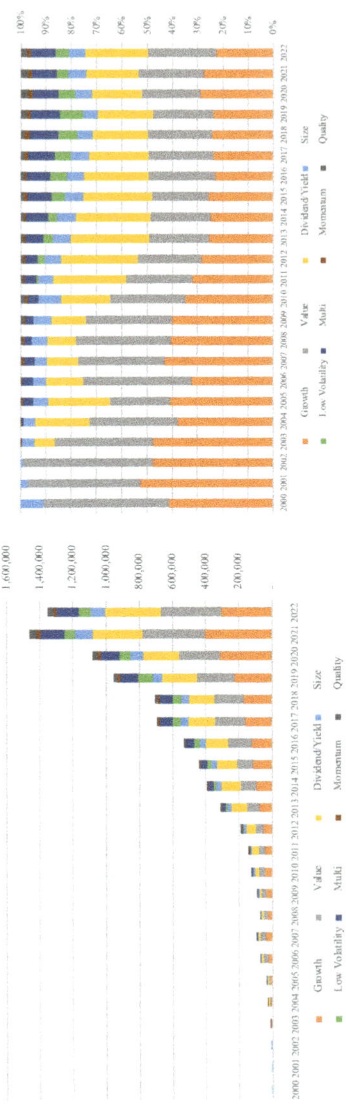

Fig. 5.6 Smart beta ETFs: AuM (*Source* Author's elaboration on Bloomberg data)

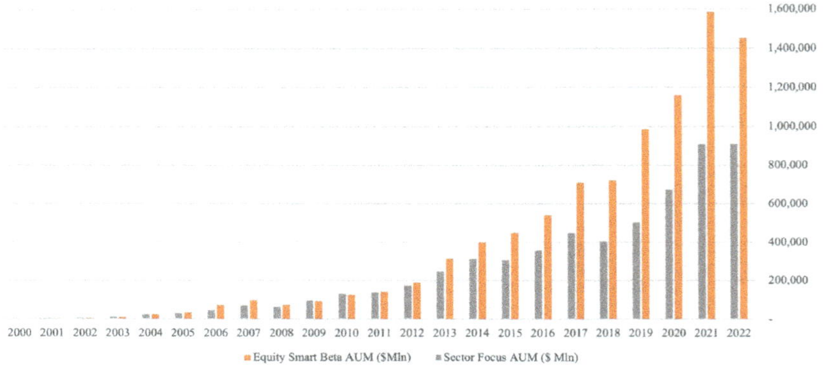

Fig. 5.7 Smart beta vs sectorial ETFs: AuM (*Source* Author's elaboration on Bloomberg data)

two types of ETF were similar in terms of interest from investors, ten years later, the preference for strategies based on factors is double compared to those based on sector allocation.

Active Exchange-Traded Funds

As widely described, ETFs have experienced unprecedented growth in popularity and in size due to their simplicity and low cost. Their goal is to invest in or replicate the performance of a basket of assets or index through a 'passive' investment strategy, i.e., automatically buying and selling based on the benchmark being tracked. The next step taken by the industry has been the search for a hybrid approach able to keep the advantages of the format of ETFs while outperforming benchmarks. In 2008, the US Securities and Exchange Commission (SEC) approved the first actively managed ETF, the Bear Stearns Current Yield Fund. The ETF was designed to provide investors with exposure to short term, high-quality fixed income securities, with the aim of generating income and preserving capital.

Active ETFs differ from traditional ETFs in that they are managed by a portfolio manager or team of managers who make investment decisions with the aim of outperforming the market. The portfolio holdings of an active ETF can change more frequently than those of a passive ETF, depending on the investment strategy being used. Thus, the portfolio manager has full discretion over the fund's investments. As a result, active ETFs tend to have higher fees than passive ETFs. Moreover, unlike Smart beta ETFs, that follow a set of predetermined rules, active ETFs rely on the subjective decisions of a portfolio manager. As a result, active ETFs tend to have higher fees than Smart beta ETFs.

Active ETFs comprise a relatively small portion of the entire $5 trillion ETF industry focused on equity. As shown in Fig. 5.8, as of December 2022, these funds contained about $215 billion, or nearly 4% of the ETF equity market.

Finally, the most recent evolution of Exchange-Traded Funds is that of *Active Non-Transparent (ANT) ETFs*. Unlike traditional ETFs, which are required to disclose their holdings on a daily basis, ANT ETFs are allowed to keep their holdings confidential, revealing them only periodically or under certain circumstances. This allows portfolio managers to maintain their investment strategies without revealing their trades to the market, which can help prevent front-running and other market impacts that can result from daily disclosure. ANT ETFs were first approved by the SEC in 2019. The SEC's approval of these ETFs followed several years of discussions and deliberations over how to structure and regulate actively managed ETFs that did not fully disclose their holdings on a daily basis. The first ANT ETFs were launched in the United States on May 2020 by major asset managers.

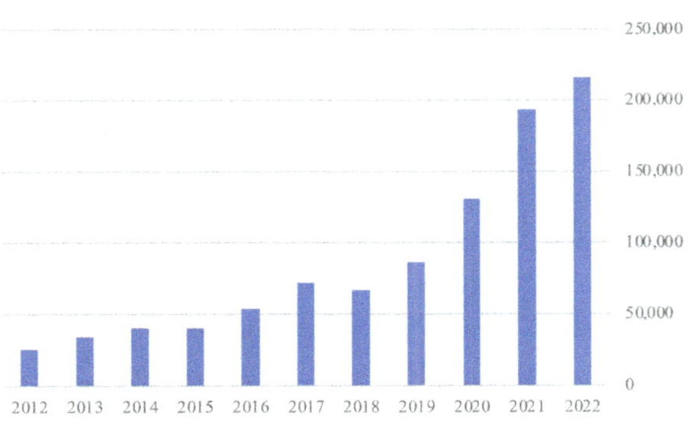

Fig. 5.8 Active ETFs: AuM (*Source* Author's elaboration on Bloomberg data)

Further Statistics

The active/passive investment line is increasingly blurred. As repeatedly stated, active management has disappointed investors' expectations with poor statistics on performance and their persistence over time. The risk management has progressively linked active management to the benchmark with a risk budget and monitoring of the tracking error volatility. The result has been a shift towards semi-active management and active bets limited to a small 'satellite' part of a portfolio that mainly mirrors the benchmark. As a consequence, we are witnessing the exponential growth of the passive management industry, first through index funds and then through ETFs. The latter, transparent and low cost, have increasingly evolved to offer investment strategies aimed at creating value by first blurring the line between active and passive management through Smart beta ETFs and then, crossing it through the recent Active ETFs. This process is clearly visible from the observation of Fig. 5.9. Over the course of 10 years, active management was about 67% of equity investing. In 2022 the statistic reversed itself, reducing to 43%. Looking at these further statistics, the advance of passive investing appears to be unstoppable.

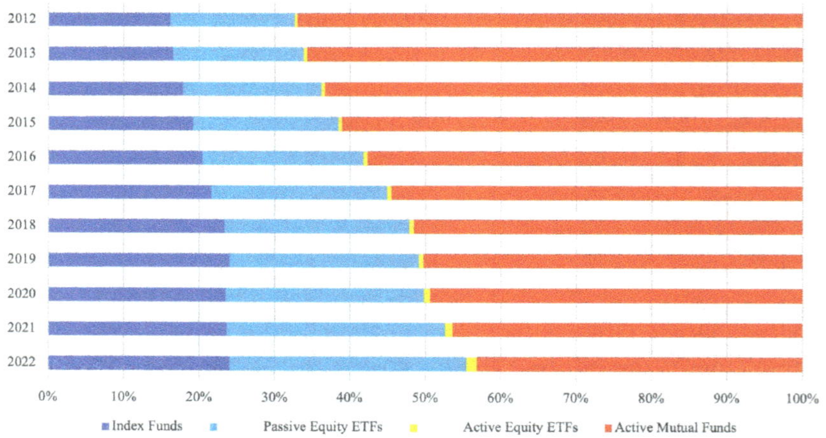

Fig. 5.9 Active vs passive investing (*Source* Author's elaboration on Bloomberg data)

References

Malkiel, B. G. (1973). *A random walk down Wall Street*. Norton.

Malkiel, B. G. (2003). The efficient market hypothesis and its critics. *Journal of Economic Perspectives, 17*(1), 59–82.

Malkiel, B. G. (2005). Reflections on the efficient market hypothesis: 30 years later. *Financial Review, 40*(1), 1–9.

CHAPTER 6

The Need for a Change: Sustainable Finance

Abstract This chapter focuses on the birth and evolution of sustainable finance. The main steps that have been taken in the last century in this sector are retraced. Over time, in fact, the perspective of investors has increasingly broadened towards assessments that go beyond the portfolio's risk and return profile and which include the principles of investment ethics. We will first focus on the steps, not only regulatory, which have been most decisive for the growth of the sector. The second part focuses on the empirical evidence of the impact of ESG integration on the assessment of financial performance and on the fundamental role of ESG disclosure as a strategic management tool for a company.

Keywords Ethical investing · Sustainable investing · Socially Responsible Investing (SRI) · ESG investing · ESG disclosure

A sustainable world needs sustainable finance. The general awareness of the significant impact of finance in making the world more sustainable can be summed up in this way: *sustainability* or sustainable development refers to the concept of meeting present needs without compromising the ability of future generations to meet their needs. It encompasses social welfare, protection of the environment, efficient use of natural

E. Bolognesi, *New Trends in Asset Management*,
https://doi.org/10.1007/978-3-031-35057-3_6

resources, and economic well-being. Thus, *sustainable finance* combines sustainability needs with economic goals.

The European Commission defines sustainable finance as the process of taking environmental, social, and governance (ESG) considerations into account when making investment decisions in the financial sector, leading to more long-term investments in sustainable economic activities and projects. In the EU's policy context, sustainable finance is understood as finance to support economic growth while reducing pressures on the environment and taking into account social and governance aspects. Sustainable finance also encompasses transparency when it comes to risks related to ESG factors that may have an impact on the financial system, and the mitigation of such risks through the appropriate governance of financial and corporate actors.

Before delving into the impact of this new investment approach on the asset management industry, it is appropriate to provide some clarifications on the terminology used over time. The term *Sustainable Investing (SI)* has evolved during the last several decades. As a result, it is a field with a substantial number of terms and acronyms, many of which are used interchangeably or defined differently by various market participants.

Fulton et al. (2012) present a timeline of the evolution of sustainable investing that helps in better understanding this field. The starting point, far into the past, is the birth of the concept of *ethical investment* which is an investment philosophy guided by moral values, ethical codes, or religious beliefs. Investment decisions include non-economic criteria which, in practice, are traditionally declined through negative (or exclusionary) screening. From the 1960s to the mid-1990s, the focus has shifted towards a broader concept of *Socially Responsible Investing (SRI)* that represents an evolution of the ethical investment approach. In its early stage, SRI was quite close to the ethical investing principles in that it allowed a level of trade-off between corporate social and financial performance when making investment decisions, and predominantly used exclusionary screening. Moreover, SRI originally emerged as a response to concerns over issues such as human rights, labour standards, and environmental degradation. The goal was to create investment strategies that align with investors' values and avoid investments in companies that engage in practices deemed harmful.

During the first half of the 2000s, SRI evolved into what is now known as *ESG investing*, which takes a broader and more systematic approach to integrating environmental, social, and governance considerations into investment decision-making. Thus, ESG investing considers not only the ethical implications of investments but also their potential impact on financial performance. More in detail, *Environmental* issues concern any aspect of a company's activity that affects the environment in a positive or negative manner. Examples include greenhouse gas emissions, renewable energy, energy efficiency, resource depletion, chemical pollution, waste management, water management, impact on biodiversity, etc. *Social* issues vary from community-related aspects, such as the improvement of health and education, to workplace-related issues, including the adherence to human rights, non-discrimination, and stakeholder engagement. Examples include labour standards (along the supply chain, child labour, forced labour), relations with local communities, talent management, controversial business practices (weapons, conflict zones), health standards, freedom of association, etc. *Governance* issues concern the quality of a company's management, culture, risk profile, and other characteristics. It includes the board accountability and their dedication towards, and strategic management of, social and environmental performance. Furthermore, it emphasises principles, such as transparent reporting and the realisation of management tasks in a manner that is essentially free of abuse and corruption. Examples include corporate governance issues (executive remuneration, shareholder rights, board structure), bribery, corruption, stakeholder dialogue, lobbying activities, etc.

Finally, the term *Responsible Investing (RI)* refers to the integration of ESG considerations into investment management processes and ownership practices in the belief that these factors can have an impact on financial performance, in particular over the medium to long term.

Sustainable Investing

Origins and Evolution

To understand the philosophy behind sustainable finance, it is necessary to retrace the main steps of its evolution. The first forms of SI date back to the early 1900s in the United States. The 1920s were the years of prohibition and it also had an effect on the allocation of savings. It dates back to 1928 when we can identify the first fund linked not only to the logic of profit maximisation. This was the Pioneer Fund, whose investment strategy was based on the purchase of shares with high intrinsic value and undervalued by the market and, at the same time, was concerned with avoiding investing in companies whose main business was linked to alcohol and tobacco. Another important influence on investment approaches was the period between the 1960s and 1970s characterised by the rise of racial equality, women's rights, consumer protection, and anti-war movements. These movements led to the creation of the first mutual funds whose policies were based on values related to faith, sensitivity to civil rights, and concern for environmental dynamics. It should be remembered that, at the end of the 1960s, the United States was engaged in the Vietnam War, a sensitive issue for both citizens and investors. Dissent to this war was on the rise across the country as the thought that investors' portfolios could profit from the war effort forced many of them to revise their investment strategies. In 1971, the first SRI fund was launched in the United States: the Pax World Fund. The aim of this fund was to provide a way for investors to align their investments with their values. Initially, the fund was focused on avoiding investments in companies that were involved in the war in Vietnam. However, over time, the fund's focus expanded to include a broader range of environmental, social, and governance (ESG) issues. In the 1990s, the fund began to gain wider recognition as interest in socially responsible investing grew. It also became one of the first mutual funds to sign on to the UN Principles for Responsible Investment (PRI) in 2007. The launch of the Pax World Fund and its success increased the momentum for this type of investment and led to the general awakening of the environmental movement in the country.

After the inception of the Pax World Fund, a series of environmental and consumer protection measures were launched, among which we recall the Clean Water Act of 1972 followed by the Endangered Species Act in 1973. Therefore, while the company was reacting to the war, to climate change, to the trafficking of human beings, and a range of political and cultural issues, even socially responsible investors followed suit by directing their investments in support of these causes. It became clear that the SRI movement, supported by investors and corporations, was intent on remaining, as well as moving forward.

The evolution of the SRI movement also continued in the 1980s, where in particular concerns for the environment and climate change began to arise in the wake of the catastrophes of Bhopal, Chernobyl, and Exxon Valdez. In 1984, the 'US Sustainable Investment Forum' (SIF) was born, and today it is one of the major resources for SRI and impact investing. The portfolio approach of the 1980s involved building a portfolio that behaved like the traditional market by avoiding investments in alcohol, tobacco, weapons, gambling, and environmental pollution. In 1984 another important socially responsible fund was born, namely the Stewardship Friend.

The 90s were characterised by a strong development of SRIs: in 1992 the Cadbury report was in fact published, the importance of which was that of having introduced the 'comply or explain principle', i.e., the principle according to which companies are required to launch a self-discipline code and must justify all the choices that deviate from these principles in the event that they decide not to respect it. In 1995, however, the first report on sustainable finance was published, 'Trend report on SRI finance', by the USSIF, and in 1999, the 'Global Sullivan Principles' were presented, a code of conduct concerning issues of respect for human rights, a code for any type of company. The popularity of SRI mutual funds continues to grow, combined with the need for a methodology able to measure and monitor the performance. Thus, in 1990 the Domini Social Index (today named MSCI KLD 400 Social Index) was launched, consisting of 400 companies listed in the United States that met certain social and environmental standards. In fact, one of the main taboos related to the issue of socially responsible investments, and which in part still persists today, is that many investors feared that these would present lower performances than traditional investments. Therefore, the construction of this index has facilitated the comparison of the risk and return profile of the portfolios built according to these principles with the traditional ones.

In the early 2000s, SRI continued to gain more and more acclaim from the public and investors, together with the introduction of important initiatives and funds. In particular, we recognise three important 'catalysts' that drove the demand for analysis of ESG performance by investors. The first concerns the heartfelt debate on the relationship between fiduciary duty and sustainability issues; the second concerns climate change; the third aims at supporting the argument that poor corporate governance is bad for markets.

In 2006, the United Nations Principles for Responsible Investment were launched with the aim of establishing guidelines for investors in integrating ESG criteria into investment practices. Socially responsible investors also seek to go beyond SRI by favouring investments that have a positive impact. This approach was strengthened in 2015 by the United

Nations Sustainable Development Goals. These goals, known as SDGs, supported by all 193 member states of the United Nations, are an urgent invitation to try to solve the challenges related to the development of the most needy areas of the world as well as address and overcome issues such as poverty, inequality, climate change, environmental degradation, peace, and justice in the world.

It is in this period that the acronym ESG also begins to be used. In fact, the birth of the ESG acronym is more recent than SRI, as the first time it was adopted was in 2006, the year of publication of the report 'Who Cares Wins'. This report underlined the centrality of the ESG theme as a driving factor for the generation of value in the long term. At the same time, a group of United Nations Environment Programme Finance Initiative (UNEP FI) asset managers together with Freshfields Bruckhaus Deringer, a leading international law firm, published a ground-breaking report titled 'A Legal Framework for the Integration of Environmental, Social and Governance Issues into Institutional Investment'. Widely referred to as the 'Freshfields Report', the landmark report argued that 'integrating ESG considerations into an investment analysis so as to more reliably predict financial performance is clearly permissible and is arguably required in all jurisdictions'. We can consider this report as one of the most effective documents for promoting the integration of ESG issues in institutional investment.

Moreover, in 2006, the famous 'Principles for Responsible Investments' (PRI) has been launched, considered a fundamental step for the integration of ESG factors in the investment selection process. In more detail, the PRI is a global initiative that aims to promote the integration of ESG factors into investment decision-making and ownership practices. The PRI is supported by a network of international signatories, including institutional investors, asset managers, and service providers. Since launching, these principles have evolved significantly as follows: (i) Growth in signatories: The PRI has experienced significant growth in signatories, with more than 4,000 signatories from over 60 countries representing over $100 trillion in assets under management, as of 2021. This growth has helped to increase the influence of the PRI and promote the integration of ESG factors in investment decision-making. (ii) Expansion of the principles: The PRI has expanded the original six principles to include more detailed guidance on how to implement responsible investment practices, as well as additional guidance for specific asset classes and investment strategies. (iii) Increased focus on climate change: The PRI has increased its focus on climate change, recognising it as a systemic risk that poses significant challenges to the long-term sustainability of the global economy. The PRI has developed specific tools and initiatives to help investors address climate change, such as the PRI's Climate Action 100+ initiative and its Net Zero Asset Owner Alliance. (iv) Emphasis on impact investing: The PRI has emphasised the importance of impact investing, which seeks to generate positive social and environmental outcomes alongside financial returns. The PRI has developed guidance for investors on how to integrate impact investing into their investment strategies. (v) Greater collaboration: The PRI has fostered greater collaboration among investors, asset managers, companies, policymakers, and civil society organisations to promote responsible investment practices and drive positive change in the global economy.

In the following years, many events took place which had a significant impact on the evolution of the sector, such as to place of ESG investment at the centre of portfolio management. In 2015, the Paris Agreement, based on the United Nations Framework Convention on Climate Change, resulted in an explosive growth of public interest in ESG with the respective further growth of social responsibility in the asset management industry. This agreement was an important milestone for companies and regulators united by clear and shared objectives. The virtuous circle created by regulation and capital markets is remarkable; significant pressure for regulatory development comes from capital markets requiring more and higher quality information for valuation purposes. EU policymakers are aware of the capital markets' role in mitigating sustainability risks and have taken an increasingly hard-line approach to implementing relevant legislation. During the same year, the UN adopted the seventeen *Sustainable Development Goals (SDGs)*, which provide a framework for sustainable development and cover issues such as poverty, education, health, and climate change. Many investors now use the SDGs as a guide for setting their ESG priorities and measuring the impact of their investments.

In 2018, the European Commission published the EU Action Plan on Sustainable Finance which is a comprehensive set of measures aimed at mobilising capital towards sustainable investments and ensuring that financial markets contribute to a more sustainable economy. The document includes a range of policy initiatives and regulatory measures that we can summarise as follows: (i) Taxonomy Regulation: This regulation provides a classification system for sustainable economic activities and helps to define what can be considered a sustainable investment. It aims to reduce the risk of 'greenwashing' and improve transparency in sustainable finance. (ii) Disclosure Regulation: This regulation requires companies and financial institutions to disclose ESG information in a standardised and comparable way. It aims to improve the transparency of ESG risks and opportunities and ensure that investors have access to reliable and relevant ESG information. (iii) Low Carbon Benchmark Regulation: This regulation requires investment managers to disclose how they integrate ESG factors into their investment decisions and to use a low carbon benchmark when managing passive funds. (iv) Green Bond Standard: The EU has developed a green bond standard that provides guidelines for issuers of green bonds, ensuring that they meet certain criteria for environmental sustainability.

Accordingly, in March 2021 the EU Sustainable Finance Disclosure Regulation (SFDR) came into force requiring asset managers and other financial firms to disclose how they integrate sustainability risks into their investment decisions and to report on the ESG performance of their products. This regulation has had a significant impact on the ESG investing landscape in Europe. Finally, we have witnessed a significant growth of *green bonds*, used to finance environmentally friendly projects. According to the Climate Bonds Initiative, the global green bond market reached $305 billion in 2020, up from $271 billion in 2019.

All of these measures represent a landmark change in the industry that stands to transform sustainable finance from an optional consideration to a focal point of the European fund industry (PwC, 2020). The impact of this epochal transformation on the asset management industry can be seen both in the flows of investments in ESG products, which grew exponentially, and in the number of funds (assets and ETFs) launched in the recent few years, exceeding 3,000 units.

ESG Factors

As already mentioned, we are seeing an exponential growth in the use of ESG principles in investment decisions. It is therefore appropriate to delve into the meaning of the individual pillars that make up the ESG approach. These three ESG pillars are, in turn, divided into several subtopics which constitute the entire architecture on the basis of which the ESG scores and ratings are implemented. Figure 6.1 shows a graphical synthesis of the topics covered by each pillar.

Fig. 6.1 ESG pillars and sub-topics (*Source* Author elaboration)

ENVIRONMENTAL—The E factor indicates how much an organisation considers the protection of natural resources. Thus, it is focused on the environmental dimension and includes both short-term risks (i.e., the increase in the price of energy goods or a particularly stringent taxonomy towards the use of fossil fuels), and long-term risks (i.e., extreme climatic events, such as prolonged periods of drought, or global warming). Furthermore, in analysing environmental risk and environmental impact, the company takes into account its entire supply chain.

Part E is divided into three subsets:

- Eco-efficiency: by eco-efficiency we mean that set of activities aimed at minimising the use of resources for each unit produced: it can be implemented, for example, through the use of recycled materials, the reduction of waste, and energy efficiency.
- Environmental impact: this issue is the most relevant, as each company, in order to be able to create stable profits in the long term,

must be aware of the risks it runs at an environmental level and their possible impact on the core business.

- Environmental management: this concerns the elaboration and disclosure of the strategies adopted to manage the environmental risks.

SOCIAL—The social pillar of ESG is wide ranging: it spans everything from diversity and inclusion to human rights, health and safety, security, ethics, and indigenous reconciliation. Pillar S includes all those aspects of social development which include both relationships with primary stakeholders and relationships with secondary stakeholders. We can identify the following issues:

- Employment: the focus is on those practices that the company adopts to ensure fair and dignified treatment of its employees. The main items in the labour dimension are: adherence to labour laws, preparation of safety protocols, fair and non-discriminatory treatment and wages, and fair trade with suppliers.
- Social development outside the company: this refers to all those projects that aim to improve the social conditions of citizens, with particular attention to developing countries. By way of example, we can include all those campaigns that aim to combat the violation of human rights, wars, regimes, and in general all situations of social unease. A particularly crucial aspect of this issue concerns the possibility that the company, while participating in numerous social development campaigns, stipulates supply contracts with companies that operate without respecting the human rights of workers and the environment. When this news becomes public knowledge, the company could suffer a huge reputational damage, as the positive activities it supports would qualify as greenwashing and the company would face heavy criticism.

GOVERNANCE—The third dimension is certainly the most impactful at the core business level, as the effects of mismanagement are tangible in both the short and long term. A wide academic literature demonstrates how an opaque policy at the level of governance has a great impact, especially during market drawdowns. In this context, the main indicators that are taken into consideration are the following:

- Level of rights, activism, and involvement of shareholders and stakeholders;
- Structure of the board of directors and its composition;
- Presence of adequate internal rules and regulations;
- Independence of the audit function, and transparency in the decision-making process of strategic operations.

ESG Disclosure

A growing number of companies are embracing ESG principles and, as a consequence, the tools available to investors and financial analysts are increasingly sophisticated. While *being* ESG-compliant has become a strategic asset, ESG disclosure is, to a greater extent, a requirement for companies of all sizes. Thus, ESG disclosure has assumed an increasing relevance in the broader Non-Financial Reporting (NFR) framework. The growing attention on sustainability and the determination of homogeneous ESG criteria is pervasive and involves issuers, investors, and regulators.

The companies' current attitude towards the ESG disclosure is the result of a voluntary strategic choice that is a response, on the one hand, to the growing stakeholders' request for transparency and, on the other, to adapt to the development of the national and supranational NFR regulation. Despite the growing attention to the improvement of disclosure, the NFR regulatory process is far from being conclusive for two reasons: (1) NFR regulation still differs substantially between geographical areas and (2) it must address the trade-off between the *stringency* of 'minimum standards' and the *flexibility* arising from 'best practices' (Jackson et al., 2020).

From this perspective, Europe stands as a global leader in ESG thanks to its strong regulatory and legislative structure. The European Union Directive 2014/95 (NFRD) on non-financial and diversity information represents an important regulatory move towards harmonising the NFR practices of all European Member States and marks a shift in NFR from a voluntary exercise to one that is mandatory for the undertakings concerned (Kinderman, 2020; La Torre et al., 2018). However, the NFRD leaves a fair amount of flexibility in the implementation of its provisions because it does not require the use of an NFR standard, nor does it impose detailed disclosure requirements (such as lists of indicators per sector). Accordingly, it gives companies significant flexibility to disclose relevant information in the way they consider most useful. As a result, companies may include a non-financial statement in their management report or, under certain conditions, prepare a separate report (European Parliamentary Research Service, 2021).

As already mentioned, the 2015 Paris Agreement has had a significant impact on ESG disclosure, particularly regarding climate-related risks and opportunities. This agreement aims to limit global warming to well below 2 degrees Celsius above pre-industrial levels and to pursue efforts to limit the temperature increase to 1.5 degrees Celsius. As a result, many investors have recognised the potential risks and opportunities associated with climate change and have started to incorporate climate-related factors into their investment decision-making processes. This has led to a growing demand for more consistent and comparable ESG disclosure. In response to this demand, a number of frameworks and initiatives have emerged that aim to improve ESG disclosure and standardisation. One such initiative is the *Task Force on Climate-related Financial Disclosures* (TCFD), which was established by the Financial Stability Board in 2015. The TCFD provides recommendations for disclosing climate-related financial risks and opportunities in a consistent and comparable manner, with the goal of improving the transparency and comparability of climate-related information. The Paris Agreement has also led to an increase in the number of companies that are disclosing their climate-related risks and opportunities. In 2015, the number of companies that reported their climate-related information through the CDP (formerly known as the Carbon Disclosure Project) was around 4,000. By 2020, this number had increased to over 9,600, representing a significant increase in ESG disclosure related to climate-related risks and opportunities.

The Impact of the ESG Integration on Financial Performance

A broad body of research focuses on the impact of ESG integration on a firm's financial performance, following different perspectives, measures, and methodologies. Research on this theme attempts to establish how social norms, markets, and institutions work individually or together in a complex process so that responsible firm behaviour converges with profitable firm behaviour (Kölbel et al., 2017).

Older academic literature, based on the agency cost theory, argues that the costs incurred by Corporate Social Responsibility (CSR) actions are additional costs and, therefore, have a negative impact on the firm's performance. In particular, Friedman (1970) stated that the only social responsibility of business is to make profits. On the one hand, if managers use corporate resources for socially responsible activities, they do so as agents fulfilling their own self-interest rather than making decisions for the benefit of shareholders. On the other hand, stakeholder theory postulates that CSR activities will result in financial gain (Jones, 1995). Later, Freeman (1984), introducing stakeholder theory of organisational management and business ethics, argues that a firm should create value for all stakeholders, not just shareholders, addressing morals and values in managing an organisation. In this view, CSR activities can alleviate conflicts of interest between companies and stakeholders and ultimately increase financial performance and corporate value (Bartlett & Preston, 2000; Cochran et al., 1985).

More recent studies demonstrate a significant value creation of ESG integration and its disclosure under multiple profiles, including: reputation improvement (Khojastehpour & Johns, 2014; Unerman, 2008); organisational attractiveness (Albinger & Freeman, 2000; Jamali et al., 2015); lower capital constraints and lower cost of capital (Cheng et al., 2014; El Ghoul et al., 2011; Francis et al., 2005); and creation of insurance-like protection (Godfrey et al., 2009).

From an accounting perspective, a vast amount of literature demonstrates that ESG activities and disclosure have a positive impact on a firm's financial performance. Dhaliwal et al. (2011) and El Ghoul et al. (2011) show that companies that initiate CSR reporting or firms with higher CSR scores enjoy a reduction in the cost of equity capital. Plumlee et al. (2015) confirm the positive relation between voluntary environmental disclosure quality and firm value in terms of expected future cash flow and cost of equity capital. Cheng et al. (2014) investigate whether CSR strategies affect the firm's ability to access finance in capital markets, confirming that higher levels of transparency reduce informational asymmetries between the firm and investors, thus mitigating perceived risk. Kim et al. (2012) argue that firms that exhibit CSR also behave in a responsible manner to constrain earnings management, thereby delivering more transparent and reliable financial information to investors. Focusing on the UK stock market, Li et al. (2018) find a positive association between ESG disclosure level and firm value (Tobin's Q), suggesting that improved transparency, accountability, and enhanced stakeholder trust play a role in boosting firm value. Still based on Tobin's Q as a proxy of firm value, Fatemi et al. (2018) demonstrate that ESG strength increases the firm value and that ESG disclosure has a negative effect, motivated by the investor's view of such disclosure as 'greenwashing'. Drempetic et al. (2019) stress the importance of ESG reporting on the ESG score. They argue that the ESG score is distorted in favour of larger companies, because ESG scores are dependent on resources for providing ESG data and data availability of the ESG score. Wong and Zhang (2022) examine the effects of adverse media coverage of ESG issues on firm-level stock performance showing that investors perceive the corporate reputation as an intangible asset to be preserved. Recently, scholars have been investigating the effects of ESG policies on financial markets without reaching a conclusive point, as the literature presents conflicting results (Khan, 2022). Moreover, as reported by Huang et al. (2022), several studies state that higher ESG performances are associated with lower risks with particular reference to systematic risk (Albuquerque et al., 2019), credit risk (Mendiratta et al., 2021), crash risk (Feng et al., 2022), downside risk (Hoepner et al., 2021), and idiosyncratic risk (He et al., 2022).

Moving to the financial markets perspective on the ESG disclosure, Dhaliwal et al. (2011) highlight that voluntary CSR disclosure is associated with increased analyst coverage, improved forecast accuracy, and reduction in forecast dispersion among firms with relatively superior CSR performance. Chung and Jo (1996) demonstrated a positive relationship between analyst coverage and corporate social performance. Wang et al. (2022) show that the quality of information disclosure improves the quality of information production by financial analysts.

Focusing on the impact of ESG disclosure on the analyst evaluations, Ioannou and Serafeim (2015) explore the relationship between CSR ratings and the sell-side analysts' assessment of US firms' future financial performance over a 15-year period. They find empirical evidence of a gradual shift from an initial unfavourable evaluation of firms with high CSR scores (motivated by the detriment of corporate profitability, i.e., agency cost) to a more optimistic evaluation (motivated by the increasing belief that CSR does not penalise a firm's financial performance and even may generate value in the long run). Luo et al. (2015) argue that analyst recommendations mediate the relationship between CSR and future stock returns. They argue that, given the growing relevance of social investing and fund managers' quest for 'investment with a conscience', more frequently firm corporate social performance is addressed as an intangible and promising asset by analysts. Bolognesi and Burchi (2023) focus on the impact of ESG disclosure scores on sell-side analysts' target prices. Focusing on the largest 3,000 US-listed firms between 2012 and 2020, they argue that the ESG disclosure is a value driver for sell-side analysts. ESG factors affect a community's long-term sustainability and serve to guide the broader financial markets, increasingly oriented towards sustainable investing. Specifically, they find that: (1) analysts recognise a premium for firms more engaged in ESG transparency (2) before the Paris Agreement this premium was mainly driven by Governance disclosure; (3) after this event this premium has also been driven by Environmental disclosure. Thus, their findings demonstrate that ESG disclosure is a strategic tool for firms to create value.

The Impact of Regulation on ESG Disclosure

In Europe, ESG disclosure has been constantly growing and, since the early 2000s, has been the subject of study by both European policymakers and national governments. The push towards the transition from voluntary towards mandatory disclosure has been gradual, with many steps being taken to draw up guidelines that could be implemented by companies belonging to different sectors.

To summarise the main steps taken in Europe in terms of NFR, we recall the European Union Directive 2014/95 on non-financial and diversity information (referred to as the 'Non-Financial Reporting Directive'). This Directive requires companies from 2018 onwards to include non-financial statements in their annual reports or in a separate filing. This includes information on environmental protection, social responsibility and treatment of employees, respect for human rights, anti-corruption and bribery, and diversity on company boards. It applies to public-interest companies with more than 500 employees, which constitutes approximately 6,000 companies and groups.

In June 2017, the European Commission (EC) provided *Guidelines on NFR* to help companies disclose relevant non-financial information in a more consistent and comparable manner. In June 2019, the EC published additional guidelines on reporting climate-related information which integrate recommendations by the Task Force on Climate-related Financial Disclosures. Moreover, in December 2019, the EC published the communication *The European Green Deal* (European Commission, 2019). This document reformulated the European commitment to tackle climate and environmental problems on a new basis, aiming at achieving the targets of the Energy and Climate Strategy, already established at the legislative level in the Clean Energy Package.

The European Green Deal presents a roadmap for making the EU's economy sustainable and aims to boost the efficient use of resources by moving to a clean, circular economy, towards averting climate change, biodiversity loss, and pollution. The European Green Deal covers all sectors of the economy, notably transportation, energy, agriculture, building construction, and infrastructure industries such as steel, cement, ICT, textiles, and chemicals. Furthermore, in 2020, the EU published the *Taxonomy Regulation* (EU 2020/852) which is a classification system that provides companies, investors, and policymakers with appropriate definitions for which economic activities can be considered environmentally sustainable. In this way, it should create security for investors, protect private investors from greenwashing, help companies to become more climate-friendly, mitigate market fragmentation, and help shift investments where they are most needed.

In the United States, the approach to ESG disclosure discipline has alternatively followed a market-based approach often referencing disclosure frameworks established by non-governmental entities to establish similar frameworks. Therefore, in the United States, sustainable investing and disclosure has been guided by voluntary, private-sector-led processes, protocols, and guidelines. More specifically, there are no mandatory ESG disclosures at the federal level. The Securities and Exchange Commission (SEC) requires all public companies to disclose information regarding human capital resources and measures or objectives if it is material to the understanding of the business. For example, in 2010, the SEC issued guidance regarding how the US securities laws and regulations may require disclosures of climate-related information, depending on a company's circumstances. However, there is general agreement that the level of information that US companies are compelled to disclose under the existing regulatory framework is significantly lower than in a number of other developed markets (EY, 2021).

To compare the dynamic of the ESG disclosure of European and US firms, we analyse the scores of the components of two broad equity market indices. We have focused on the Bloomberg Europe Large, Mid, & Small Cap Index because it covers approximately 99% of the investable European markets, including 1,910 firms. For the United States, we have selected the Russell 3000 Index because it covers about 98% of the investable US equity market and constitutes 3,020 firms. The observation period is 2012–2020. For ESG disclosure we have used scores provided by Bloomberg. Composite ESG scores range from 0.1 for companies that disclose a minimum amount of ESG data to 100 for those that disclose every data point collected by Bloomberg. Each data point is weighted in terms of importance. The overall score is also tailored to different industry sectors. The score measures the amount of ESG data a firm publicly reports. We also use the same approach for testing separate E, S, and G scores.

Figure 6.2 shows the dynamics of both the overall ESG score and the three pillars. We can at first notice an overall increase in the median values of the scores and a reduction in their interquartile distance. Moreover, the comparison between the two samples shows significantly different dynamics. In fact, in Europe, average disclosure scores are higher than in the United States. Furthermore, the growing trend in Europe is constant and noticeable. Looking in more detail at the data on US disclosure, a greater lack of homogeneity with respect to the European ones is evident. In particular, the significant number of outliers for each pillar is surprising at first. Furthermore, the difference between disclosure in governance compared to the other pillars is evident; in this case the values are significantly higher, indicating a greater culture towards this issue than environmental and social concerns.

This evidence demonstrates that Europe and the United States have taken different paths towards sustainability reporting. This is largely the result of differences in governance, regulatory culture, and the balancing of domestic interests: European companies showing significant qualitative and quantitative improvement in their ESG disclosures compared to US companies. This difference is likely attributable to the regulatory context that progressively has become increasingly structured and stringent for European companies.

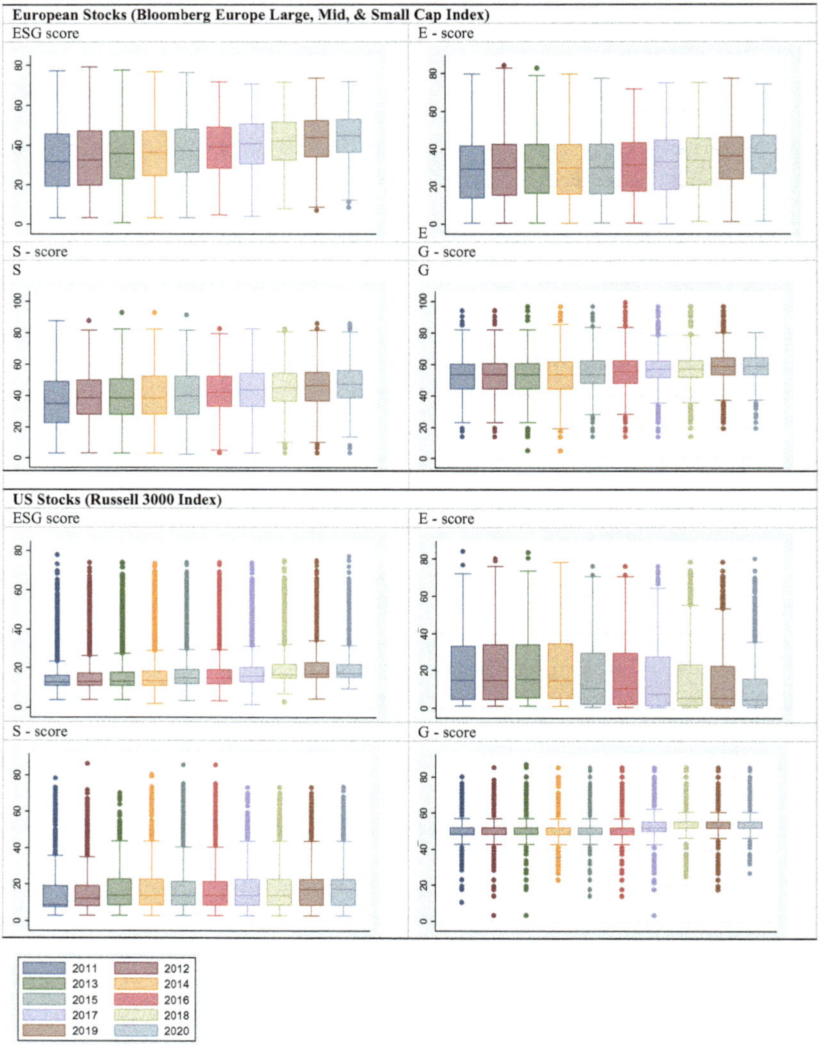

Fig. 6.2 Boxplot visualisation of ESG disclosure scores by year (*Source* Author's computation on Bloomberg data)

References

Albinger, H. S., & Freeman, S. J. (2000). Corporate social performance and attractiveness as an employer to different job seeking populations. *Journal of Business Ethics, 28*(3), 243–253.

Albuquerque, R., Koskinen, Y., & Zhang, C. (2019). Corporate social responsibility and firm risk: Theory and empirical evidence. *Management Science, 65*(10), 4451–4469.

Bartlett, A., & Preston, D. (2000). Can ethical behaviour really exist in business. *Journal of Business Ethics, 23*, 199–209.

Bolognesi, E., & Burchi, A. (2023). The impact of the ESG disclosure on sell-side analysts' target prices: The new era post Paris agreements. *Research in International Business and Finance, 64*, 101827.

Cheng, B., Ioannou, I., & Serafeim, G. (2014). Corporate social responsibility and access to finance. *Strategic Management Journal, 35*(1), 1–23.

Chung, K. H., & Jo, H. (1996). The impact of security analysts' monitoring and marketing functions on the market value of firms. *Journal of Financial and Quantitative Analysis, 31*, 493–512.

Cochran, P. L., Wood, R. A., & Jones, T. B. (1985). The composition of boards of directors and incidence of golden parachutes. *Academy of Management Journal, 28*, 664–671.

Dhaliwal, D. S., Li, O. Z., Tsang, A., & Yang, Y. G. (2011). Voluntary nonfinancial disclosure and the cost of equity capital: The initiation of corporate social responsibility reporting. *The Accounting Review, 86*(1), 59–100.

Drempetic, S., Klein, C., & Zwergel, B. (2019). The influence of firm size on the ESG score: Corporate sustainability ratings under review. *Journal of Business Ethics, 167*, 333–360.

El Ghoul, S., Guedhami, O., Kwok, C. C. Y., & Mishra, D. R. (2011). Does corporate social responsibility affect the cost of capital? *Journal of Banking & Finance, 35*(9), 2388–2406.

European Commission. (2019). *The European Green Deal.*

European Parliamentary Research Service. (2021). *Non-financial Reporting Directive.*

EY. (2021). *The future of sustainability reporting standards. The policy evolution and the actions companies can take today.*

Fatemi, A., Glaum, M., & Kaiser, S. (2018). ESG performance and firm value: The moderating role of disclosure. *Global Finance Journal, 38*, 45–64.

Feng, J., Goodell, J. W., & Shen, D. (2022). ESG rating and stock price crash risk: Evidence from China. *Finance Research Letters, 46*, 102476.

Francis, J. R., Khurana, I. K., & Pereira, R. (2005). Disclosure incentives and effects on cost of capital around the world. *The Accounting Review, 80*, 1125–1162.

Freeman, R. E. (1984). *Strategic management: A stakeholder approach*. Cambridge University Press.

Friedman, M. (1970). A Friedman doctrine: The social responsibility of business is to increase its profits. *The New York times Magazine, 13*, 32–33.

Fulton, M., Kahn, B., & Sharples, C. (2012). *Sustainable investing: Establishing long-term value and performance*. Deutsche Bank Climate Change Investment Research.

Godfrey, P. C., Merrill, C. B., & Hansen, J. M. (2009). The relationship between corporate social responsibility and shareholder value: An empirical test of the risk management hypothesis. *Strategic Management Journal, 30*(4), 425–445.

He, F., Qin, S., Liu, Y., Wu, J. G. (2022). CSR and idiosyncratic risk: Evidence from ESG information disclosure. *Finance Research Letters*, 102936.

Hoepner, A. G. F., Oikonomou, I., Sautner, Z., Starks, L. T., & Zhou, X., (2021). *ESG shareholder engagement and downside risk* (SSRN Scholarly Paper No. 2874252). Social Science Research Network.

Huang, W., Luo, Y., Wang, X., & Xiao, L. (2022). Controlling shareholder pledging and corporate ESG behavior. *Research in International Business and Finance, 61*, 101655.

Ioannou, I., & Serafeim, G. (2015). The impact of corporate social responsibility on investment recommendations: Analysts' perceptions and shifting institutional logics. *Strategic Management Journal, 36*(7), 1053–1081.

Jackson, G., Bartosch, J., Avetisyan, E., Kinderman, D., & Knudsen, J. S. (2020). Mandatory non-financial disclosure and its influence on CSR: An international comparison. *Journal of Business Ethics, 162*(2), 323–342.

Jamali, D. R., El Dirani, A. M., & Harwood, I. A. (2015). Exploring human resource management roles in corporate social responsibility: The CSR-HRM co-creation model. *Business Ethics: A European Review, 24*(2), 125–143.

Jones, T. M. (1995). Instrumental stakeholder theory: A synthesis of ethics and economics. *Academy of Management Review, 20*(2), 404–437.

Khan, M. A. (2022). ESG disclosure and firm performance: A bibliometric and meta analysis. *Research in International Business and Finance, 61*, 101668.

Khojastehpour, M., & Johns, R. (2014). The effect of environmental CSR issues on corporate/brand reputation and corporate profitability. *European Business Review*.

Kim, Y., Park, M. S., & Wier, B. (2012). Is earnings quality associated with corporate social responsibility? *The Accounting Review, 87*, 761–796.

Kinderman, D. (2020). The challenges of upward regulatory harmonization: The case of sustainability reporting in the European Union. *Regulation & Governance, 14*(4), 674–697.

Kölbel, J. F., Busch, T., & Jancso, L. M. (2017). How media coverage of corporate social irresponsibility increases financial risk. *Strategic Management Journal, 38*(11), 2266–2284.

La Torre, M., Sabelfeld, S., Blomkvist, M., Tarquinio, L., & Dumay, J. (2018). Harmonising non-financial reporting regulation in Europe: Practical forces and projections for future research. *Meditari Accountancy Research, 26*, 598–621.

Li, Y., Gong, M., Zhang, X.-Y., & Koh, L. (2018). The impact of environmental, social, and governance disclosure on firm value: The role of CEO power. *The British Accounting Review, 50*(1), 60–75.

Luo, X., Wang, H., Raithel, S., & Zheng, Q. (2015). Corporate social performance, analyst stock recommendations, and firm future returns. *Strategic Management Journal, 36*(1), 123–136.

Mendiratta, R., Varsani, H. D., & Giese, G. (2021). How ESG affected corporate credit risk and performance. *The Journal of Impact and ESG Investing, 2*(2), 101–116.

Plumlee, M., Brown, D., Hayes, R. M., & Marshall, R. S. (2015). Voluntary environmental disclosure quality and firm value: Further evidence. *Journal of Accounting and Public Policy, 34*(4), 336–361.

PwC Luxemburg. (2020). *2022: The growth opportunity of the century*. Sustainable Finance Series.

Unerman, J. (2008). Strategic reputation risk management and corporate social responsibility reporting. *Accounting, Auditing & Accountability Journal*.

Wang, F., Mbanyele, W., & Muchenje, L. (2022). Economic policy uncertainty and stock liquidity: The mitigating effect of information disclosure. *Research in International Business and Finance, 59*, 101533.

Wong, J. B., & Zhang, Q. (2022). Stock market reactions to adverse ESG disclosure via media channels. *The British Accounting Review, 54*, 101045.

CHAPTER 7

The Next Challenge: ESG and CLIMATE Investing

Abstract This chapter focuses on the most recent investment approaches dictated by investors' growing awareness of the positive impact that finance can have on sustainability and climate change mitigation. We will first focus on ESG investing and on the main tool available to the manager for defining the portfolio, i.e., the ESG ratings. A description of the main rating providers will be provided, emphasising the problem of divergence in ratings as well as the size effect. The main sustainable investment strategies will then be listed. We will therefore focus on climate investing, briefly listing the European regulatory process that led to the sudden development of this investment philosophy. Finally, we will focus on the ESG and climate indices and on the risk and return profiles of a sample of these indices.

Keywords ESG ratings · ESG Investing · ESG Indexing · Climate Investing · Climate Indexing

Structural and systematic shifts, such as climate change, resource scarcity, regulatory pressures, and the importance of human capital and diversity, increasingly pose material business risks and, simultaneously, present opportunities to issuers and investors globally. Consequently, numerous investors use ESG information because of client demand or as part of their

E. Bolognesi, *New Trends in Asset Management*,
https://doi.org/10.1007/978-3-031-35057-3_7

product development process. As the investor community continues to signal more interest in sustainability and ESG data, the value of external, third-party ratings has increased. These ratings, prepared for individual companies, are intended to be used by investors to evaluate their portfolios, by sustainability professionals for benchmarking against peers, and by sell-side financial analysts for their companies' forecasts.

ESG investing is gaining traction as investors increasingly seek long-term value and alignment with sustainability and climate-related objectives. Asset managers globally are expected to increase their ESG-related assets under management (AuM) to US$33.9tn by 2026, from US$18.4tn in 2021 (PwC, 2020). With a projected compound annual growth rate of 12.9%, ESG assets are on track to constitute 21.5% of total global AuM in less than five years. It represents a dramatic and continuing shift in the asset and wealth management industry. The report also captures the views of 250 institutional investors and asset managers worldwide, representing nearly half of global AuM. Consistently, investors' preferences for an ESG strategy continued to drive inflows in actively managed ESG funds, while their non-ESG actively managed counterparts continued to experience outflows (Deloitte, 2022).

ESG Investing

ESG Ratings: Main Actors and Methodologies

ESG ratings are based on a materiality framework that measures a company's exposure to industry-specific material ESG and how well a company is managing those ESG risks. In other words, ESG ratings provide a score on ESG sustainability, and therefore they are not linked to a purely financial measurement. ESG ratings first emerged in the 1980s as a way for investors to screen companies on ESG performance. EIRIS (Ethical Investment Research Services) is one of the earliest ESG rating agencies, having been founded in 1983. EIRIS was initially focused on providing research and analysis to socially responsible investors, and later expanded its services to include ESG ratings of companies. Since then, the market for ESG ratings has grown exponentially, especially in the past decade. Because ESG ratings are an essential basis for most kinds of sustainable investing, the market for ESG ratings grew in parallel to sustainable investing.

The number of ESG standards and frameworks, data providers, ratings, and rankings has expanded over time, with more than 600 ESG ratings and rankings existing globally as of 2018 and continuing to grow since then (SustainAbility, 2020). In 2023, Bloomberg estimates 1,100 ESG data providers worldwide. In recent years, major rating agencies have purchased large stakes in ESG rating agencies, understanding the strong synergies arising from the integration of the two activities and the strong growth potential of the sector. As an example, in 2019 Moody's has acquired the majority of Vigeo EIRIS while S&P has acquired RobecoSAM, two leading companies in the ESG rating framework. It's worth noting that RobecoSAM includes the Corporate Sustainability Assessment (CSA) division, whose algorithms form the basis of the popular Dow Jones Sustainability Index.

Here we focus on the main raters in this sector which are also used for the construction of sustainable and ESG indexes. It is appropriate to briefly dwell on the general evaluation criteria and methodologies that they adopt, without any claim to completeness:

- Sustainalytics;
- MSCI ESG Research;
- Bloomberg ESG Scores;
- FTSE Russell's ESG Ratings;
- ISS ESG.
- Refinitiv ESG Scores

SUSTAINALYTICS is controlled by Morningstar group which uses the data produced by its agency for the construction of the Morningstar Sustainability Rating. The Sustainalytics approach is built with the aim of highlighting the most relevant ESG risks for a company. Sustainalytics' ESG Risk Ratings measure a company's exposure to industry-specific material ESG risks and how well a company is managing those risks. This multi-dimensional way of measuring ESG risk combines the concepts of management and exposure to arrive at an absolute assessment of ESG risk. Sustainalytics identifies five categories of ESG risk severity that could impact a company's enterprise value: negligible, low, medium, high, and severe and represented by the popular ESG Globes icon. These scores are then used by Morningstar for the formation of its ratings, which are constructed through a normalisation at sector level, which aims to avoid distortions that would prevent the investor from understanding how much more or less ESG a company was compared to peers.

The *MSCI ESG Research* Division has been established in 2013 and is responsible for providing reports and tools for analysing ESG factors. In its rating methodology, MSCI follows a value-based approach, that evolved, over time, thanks to the influence of the many companies that have been acquired, from an initially strongly quantitative approach. Specifically, the MSCI ESG rating is an average of the scores obtained in the three different areas, which are an expression of the evaluation of thirty-five different key factors. These scores are then calculated, taking into account the sector, the time horizon in which the risk could materialise the possible economic impact, and are subsequently aggregated by reference area. The overall ESG score will therefore be an arithmetic mean of the scores for E, S, and G pillars. The MSCI ESG rating is similar to the main non-ESG rating agencies, ranging from AAA to CCC. Thus, we can identify the leaders as (AAA and AA), the average (A, BBB, BB), and the laggard (B, CCC).

BLOOMBERG ESG SCORES. In 2020, Bloomberg has launched its proprietary ESG scores, calculated using a methodology that incorporates company-reported data, as well as third-party data sources. The rating of each pillar is an expression of the grouping of different topics, which in turn are divided into fields. Depending on the industry, Bloomberg includes or excludes different fields, to improve comparability. The various fields are given a score ranging from 1 to 10 (where 10 is the best score). For the weighting of these factors in a theme, a calculation is made that considers three different variables, which are: (1) Probability: a probability of completion has been assigned to each field which can be low, medium, or high; (2) Severity: each field is assigned a high, medium, or low severity depending on the potential loss should that risk materialise; (3) Time horizon: each field is assigned a score according to the time horizon of the risk: low risk (5–10 years), medium risk (2–5 years), and high risk (2 years). As reported by Bloomberg, the long-term time horizon usually concerns physical risks, the medium-term one usually concerns regulatory risks. Once the score of the various topics has been calculated, they are corrected for the disclosure, which adds a point if adequately present. Once the various topics have been calculated, they are grouped into the different areas, and are weighted differently for each sector. Once these scores have been calculated, their arithmetic mean leads to the formation of the ESG score.

FTSE RUSSELL ESG RATINGS aims to synthesise ESG information (both qualitative and quantitative) objectively into a single score; it combines an issuer's total ESG exposure and performance in multiple dimensions. The final score attributed to any organisation rests on assessments conducted for the three E, S, and G pillars, covering fourteen themes, themselves spread over 300 indicators. Once the two scores have been calculated for each indicator that is part of a relevant topic (those with negligible exposure are excluded), a matrix is created which has the task of providing the aggregate score of the topic. The issues are then grouped by the area to which they belong and the ESG score will also be an arithmetic mean of the value of these three pillars. The ESG score provided by FTSE Russell ranges from 1 to 5.

REFINITIV ESG Scores are designed to measure a company's relative ESG performance, commitment, and effectiveness based on company-reported data. This rating covers ten main themes including emissions, environmental product innovation, human rights, shareholders, and so on. It also provides an overall ESG combined (ESGC) score, which is discounted for significant ESG controversies impacting the corporations we cover. The percentile rank scores are available in both percentages and letter grades from D- to A + . They are benchmarked against The Refinitiv Business Classifications (TRBC—Industry Group) for all environmental and social categories, as well as the controversies score. They are also measured against the country of incorporation for all governance categories. The ESG scores are data-driven, accounting for the most material industry metrics, with minimal company size and transparency biases. The scores are based on the relative performance of ESG factors with the company's sector (for environmental and social) and country of incorporation (for governance). Refinitiv's ESG scoring methodology has the following key calculation principles: (1) ESG magnitude (materiality) weightings; (2) Company disclosure; (3) ESG controversies overlay; (4) Industry and country benchmarks at the data point scoring level, to facilitate comparable analysis within peer groups; (5) Percentile rank scoring methodology, to eliminate hidden layers of calculations. This methodology produces a score between 0 and 100, as well as easy-to-understand letter grades.

ESG Ratings: Diverging Evaluations and Size Effect

As already mentioned, in 2023 we can count over 1,100 ESG data providers worldwide. As a consequence, ESG ratings are not standardised and different providers may have different rating systems, which can lead to significant variations in the assessments of the same company.

Berg et al. (2022) argue that ESG rating agencies allow investors to screen companies for ESG performance, like credit ratings allow investors to screen companies for creditworthiness. However, they recognise at least three important differences between ESG ratings and credit ratings. First, while creditworthiness is relatively clearly defined as the probability of default, the definition of ESG performance is less evident. It is a concept based on values that are diverse and evolving. Thus, an important part of the service that ESG rating agencies offer is an interpretation of what ESG performance means. Second, while financial reporting standards have matured and converged over the past century, ESG reporting is in its infancy. There are competing reporting standards for ESG disclosure, many of which are voluntary or limited to single jurisdictions, giving corporations broad discretion regarding whether and what to report. Thus, ESG ratings provide a service to investors by collecting and aggregating information from across a spectrum of sources and reporting standards. These two differences explain why the divergence between ESG ratings is so much more pronounced than the divergence between credit ratings, the latter being correlated at 99%. Third, ESG raters are paid by investors who use the ratings, not by the companies that are rated, as is the case with credit raters. As a result, the problem of rating shopping, which has been discussed as a potential reason for credit ratings diverging, does not apply to ESG rating providers. In their analysis, the authors focus on six different raters (KLD, Sustainalytics, Moody's ESG, S&P Global, Refinitiv, and MSCI) and demonstrate that ESG ratings from different providers disagree substantially, where the correlations range between from 0.38 to 0.71.

Therefore, ESG raters, by not analysing purely quantitative aspects, have the possibility of giving a subjective weight to the various factors analysed, over or underweighting the importance of the variables considered and including or excluding certain aspects, which they could deem not worthy of consideration or misleading. This disagreement has important consequences. First, it makes it difficult to evaluate the ESG performance of companies, funds, and portfolios, which is the primary purpose of ESG ratings. Second, ESG rating divergence could discourage firms from improving their ESG performance.

The lack of homogeneity in the ESG ratings must be added the problem deriving from the empirical evidence of the positive correlation between ESG ratings and company size. Academic literature has widely highlighted this side effect. Drempetic et al. (2019) support this correlation with the evidence that larger companies usually show greater disclosure and can produce the data required by the rating agencies with lower costs. This effort leads to higher ratings than those of smaller competitors. In fact, whenever data are not available, rating agencies assume the worst-case scenario instead of an average scenario, a choice defined as a 'non-trust system'. In support of this thesis, there is also the tendency for public institutions to carry out studies that significantly overweight the impacts of large companies as the data are more easily available and reliable. For this reason, especially when the agencies use only public data, the effect of a greater number of data for large companies would be even more significant.

Still focusing on the positive correlation between size and ESG scores, on a theoretical level, we can provide explanations: in the first place, as mentioned above, larger companies can be better organised to obtain more data, which makes them 'more ESG' than the smaller, on average. Secondly, it is easy to understand how, the larger a company is, the more it is subject to external pressures: both local and national politics often turn to businesses to adopt policies aimed at the social and environmental improvement of the particular territory in which they are located.

Responsible Investment Strategies

Sustainable and responsible investments can be declined according to alternative strategies, each of which is characterised by specific objectives and methodologies. According to Eurosif, we can describe these strategies as follows:

Best-in-class: An approach where leading or best-performing investments within a universe, category, or class are selected or weighted based on ESG criteria. This approach involves the selection or weighting of the best-performing or most improved companies or assets as identified by ESG analysis, within a defined investment universe. This approach includes 'Best-in-class', 'Best-in-universe', and 'Best-effort'.

Engagement & voting: Engagement activities and active ownership through voting of shares and engagement with companies on ESG matters. This is a long-term process, seeking to influence behaviour or increase disclosure. Engagement and voting on corporate governance only is necessary, but not sufficient to be counted in this strategy.

ESG integration: The explicit inclusion by asset managers of ESG risks and opportunities into traditional financial analysis and investment decisions based on a systematic process and appropriate research sources. This type covers explicit consideration of ESG factors alongside financial factors in the mainstream analysis of investments. The integration process focuses on the potential impact of ESG issues on company financials (positive and negative), which in turn may affect the investment decision.

Exclusions: An approach that excludes specific investments or classes of investment from the investible universe such as companies, sectors, or countries. This approach systematically excludes companies, sectors, or countries from the permissible investment universe if involved in certain activities based on specific criteria. Common criteria include weapons, pornography, tobacco, and animal testing. Exclusions can be applied at individual fund or mandate level, but increasingly also at asset manager or asset owner level, across the entire product range of assets. This approach is also referred to as ethical- or values-based exclusions, as exclusion criteria are typically based on the choices made by asset managers or asset owners.

Impact investing: Impact investments are investments made into companies, organisations, and funds with the intention to generate social and environmental impact alongside a financial return. Impact investments can be made in both emerging and developed markets, and target a range of returns from below market-to-market rate, depending upon the circumstances. Investments are often project-specific, and distinct from philanthropy, as the investor retains ownership of the asset and expects a positive financial return. Impact investment includes microfinance, community investing, and social business/entrepreneurship funds.

Norms-based screening: Screening of investments according to their compliance with international standards and norms. This approach involves the screening of investments based on international norms or combinations of norms covering ESG factors. International norms on ESG are those defined by international bodies such as the United Nations (UN).

Sustainability themed. Investment in themes or assets linked to the development of sustainability. Thematic funds focus on specific or multiple issues related to ESG. Sustainability-themed investments inherently contribute to addressing social and/or environmental challenges such as climate change, eco-efficiency, and health. Funds are required to have an ESG analysis or screen of investments in order to be counted in this approach.

ESG Investing and Regulation

As already mentioned, in Europe, ESG investing has been supported by an intense regulatory process. In Fig. 7.1 we summarise the main step of the European framework on sustainable finance with a particular emphasis on those more impactful from the asset management industry. We firstly recall, from Chapter 6, the 2014 Non-Financial Reporting Directive (NFRD) as an important regulatory move towards harmonising the disclosure practices of all European Member States. On December 2015, the Paris Agreement set out a global framework to avoid dangerous climate change by limiting global warming to well below 2 °C and pursuing efforts to limit it to 1.5 °C. In March 2018, the European Commission published an 'Action Plan for sustainable finance', defining the strategy for the creation of a financial system for the promotion of sustainable development from an economic, social, and environmental point of view, which may help the implementation of the Paris Agreement on Climate Change and the United Nations 2030 Agenda for Sustainable Development.

On 11 December 2019, the European Commission announced the European Green Deal to transform the European Union into a modern, resource-efficient, and competitive economy. The European Green Deal provides a roadmap with actions to boost the efficient use of resources by moving to a clean, circular economy and stop climate change, reverse biodiversity loss, and cut pollution. It outlines investments needed and financing tools available and explains how to ensure a just and inclusive transition. The European Green Deal covers all sectors of the economy, notably transport, energy, agriculture, buildings, and industries such as steel, cement, ICT, textiles, and chemicals. The goal is to reach a climate-neutral economy in the EU by 2050, with a reduction of 55% already implemented in 2030. To achieve these climate goals, the Green Deal includes an investment plan of 1 trillion euros over the next 10 years.

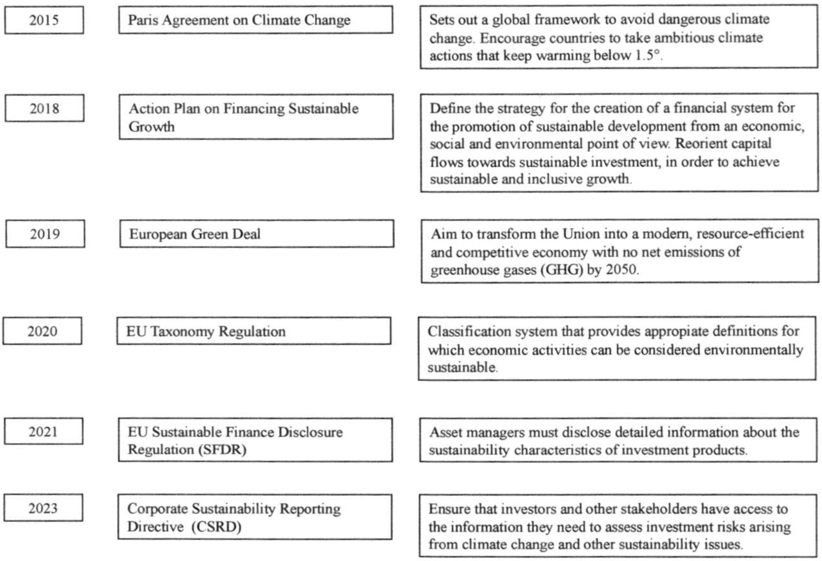

Fig. 7.1 EU regulatory framework on sustainable finance: A timeline (*Source* Author's elaboration)

Despite this huge investment, the EU depends also on the support of the private sector to achieve the Paris climate agreement. To reach these targets, further regulations have followed which have had an impact on the asset management industry. First, one of the cornerstones of the Green Deal is to bring clarity to the market regarding which economic activities can be considered sustainable with the aim of encouraging sustainable investing and preventing greenwashing. The EU Taxonomy is an ambitious attempt to define these activities and the related technical standards for six environmental objectives (see the following section on Climate Investing). The Taxonomy Regulation was published in the *Official Journal of the European Union* on 22 June 2020 and entered into force on 12 July 2020.

Moreover, the EU Sustainable Finance Disclosure Regulation (SFDR) came into effect in March 2021. This regulation requires asset managers to disclose detailed information about the sustainability characteristics of their investment products, including how ESG factors are integrated into investment decision-making processes, and how the products align with specific sustainability objectives. The SFDR applies to all financial market participants that offer financial products within the European Union, regardless of whether they are based in the EU or not. Thus, the SFDR aims to increase transparency and improve the comparability of ESG-related information provided by financial market participants, including asset managers, investment funds, and investment advisors.

To briefly sum up the key impacts of SFDR on asset management, we mention:

- Increased transparency: SFDR requires asset managers to provide greater transparency on the sustainability characteristics of their investment products. This includes disclosing the degree to which ESG factors are considered in the investment process and the impact of investment decisions on sustainability factors.
- Improved comparability: SFDR requires standardised disclosure of sustainability information, which should make it easier for investors to compare investment products based on ESG criteria.
- Enhanced due diligence: Asset managers are required to carry out due diligence on the sustainability risks and impacts of their investments and disclose how they manage these risks. This could result in more robust ESG policies and procedures.
- A shift towards sustainable investments: As investors increasingly demand sustainable investment products, asset managers may need to develop new products or adapt existing ones to meet this demand.
- Potential impact on performance: The SFDR may also have an impact on the performance of investment products, as asset managers may need to consider ESG factors when making investment decisions, which could affect portfolio composition and returns.

Furthermore, on 5 January 2023, the Corporate Sustainability Reporting Directive (CSRD) entered into force. This new directive modernises and strengthens the rules concerning the social and environmental information that companies have to report. A broader set of large companies, as well as listed SMEs, will now be required to report on sustainability—approximately 50,000 companies in total. The aim of these new rules is to ensure that investors and other stakeholders have access to the information they need to assess investment risks arising from climate change and other sustainability issues. Finally, reporting costs will be reduced for companies over the medium to long term by harmonising the information that is to be provided. The first companies will have to apply the new rules for the first time in the 2024 financial year, for reports published in 2025.

Climate Investing

Climate investing refers to the investment in companies, projects, and technologies that are focused on reducing the negative impact of climate change. This includes investments in renewable energy, energy efficiency, clean technology, sustainable transportation, and other initiatives that contribute to the reduction of greenhouse gas emissions and the transition to a low-carbon economy. Climate investing is driven by the recognition that climate change poses significant risks to the global economy and society, and that urgent action is required to mitigate these risks. The investment community is increasingly focused on climate investing as a way to align financial returns with environmental and social goals.

As already mentioned, European regulation has exerted pressure to develop this new investment approach and, as a consequence, has led to increasing attention given to environmental objectives in investment choices and processes. In particular, the EU Taxonomy regulation describes a framework to classify 'green' or 'sustainable' economic activities executed in the EU. Previously, there was no clear definition of green, sustainable, or environmentally friendly economic activity. Compared to their competitors, sustainable companies stand out positively and thus should benefit from higher investments. More in detail, the focus of the taxonomy lies in the six environmental objectives (see Fig. 7.2).

To be classified as a sustainable economic activity according to the EU Taxonomy, a company must not only contribute to at least one environmental objective but also must not violate the remaining ones. An activity aiming to mitigate the climate but, at the same time, also negatively affecting biodiversity cannot be classified as sustainable. The classification of an economic activity in terms of sustainability is based

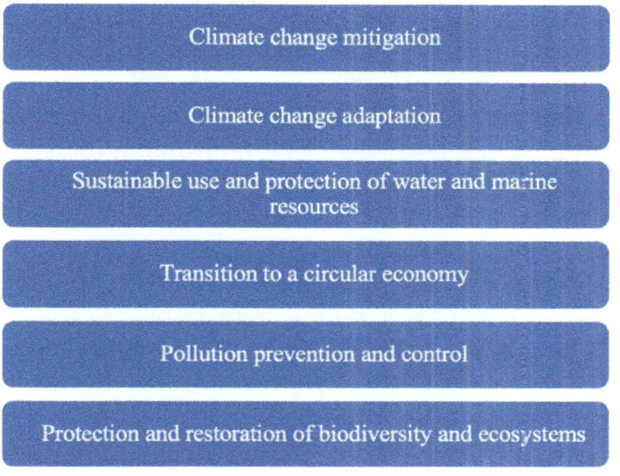

Fig. 7.2 EU Taxonomy: Environmental objectives (*Source* Author's elaboration)

on the following four criteria, which refer to the previously mentioned environmental objectives:

- The economic activity contributes to one of the six environmental objectives.
- The economic activity does 'no significant harm' to any of the six environmental objectives.
- The economic activity meets 'minimum safeguards' such as the UN Guiding Principles on Business and Human Rights to avoid a negative social impact.
- The economic activity complies with the technical screening criteria developed by the EU Technical Expert Group.

It is clear that the EU Taxonomy is closely related to climate finance, as the former is designed to provide a framework for identifying sustainable economic activities, including those related to climate change mitigation and adaptation, and the latter is designed to provide financial resources for such activities. In other words, the EU Taxonomy can help investors and asset managers to identify sustainable investment opportunities, and climate finance can provide the necessary resources to fund those opportunities. In addition, the EU Taxonomy can help policymakers to design effective policies and regulations that encourage investment in sustainable economic activities and support the transition to a low-carbon economy.

Climate investing can take many forms, including investing in companies that are actively working to reduce their carbon footprint, investing in renewable energy projects such as wind and solar farms, or investing in innovative technologies that help reduce carbon emissions. A low-carbon footprint means that the portfolio has a low exposure to carbon-intensive companies. 'Carbon intensity' is a measurement of the carbon dioxide and other greenhouse gases released annually by a company at a given time, in relation to the revenue of the company. In other words, it shows how carbon efficient the company is. Thus, a portfolio's carbon intensity is a weighted average of carbon intensities of companies which constitute the fund.

In particular, the greenhouse gas accounting has grown in importance; the industry has classified all emissions into three scopes:

1. *Scope 1* emissions refer to direct emissions from sources that are owned or controlled by a company. This includes emissions from company-owned vehicles, manufacturing facilities, and other operations that are directly under the control of the company.
2. *Scope 2* emissions refer to indirect emissions from the generation of electricity, heat, or steam that is purchased by a company. This includes emissions from power plants or other sources of electricity used by the company, but not owned or controlled by the company.
3. *Scope 3* emissions refer to all other indirect emissions that are not included in Scope 2. This includes emissions from the supply chain, employee commuting, and product use by customers. Scope 3 emissions are often the largest and most difficult to measure and manage.

Understanding Scope 1, 2, and 3 emissions is important for ESG investors because it provides a more comprehensive picture of a company's environmental impact. By considering all three scopes, investors can better assess a company's exposure to climate-related risks and opportunities, and make more informed investment decisions. Companies that are actively working to reduce their greenhouse gas emissions across all three scopes are generally considered to be leaders in sustainability and may be attractive investment opportunities for climate investing.

New Frontiers on Indexation

As can be easily understood, the asset management industry has promptly declined the new principles of sustainable investment through new market indexes. Going back in time, the first ESG index, the Domini 400 Social Index (now the MSCI KLD 400 Social Index), was launched by KLD Research & Analytics in 1990. The governance of the KLD 400 index has historically been maintained by a committee that has acted on the basis of considerations such as ESG, size, and sector weighting, as well as the evolution of investors' perspectives on ESG issues. Today, rather than relying on a committee, the KLD 400 is governed by a transparent set of quantitative rules that relate to ESG ratings, ESG dispute scores, targets for related sector representation, and the handling of corporate events. It is rebalanced quarterly and constituents are capitalisation weighted. With a track record spanning over 28 years, the KLD 400 is widely cited in the academic literature examining the impact of sustainable investing on financial performance. The evolution of the KLD 400 illustrates how ESG indices have led to improvements in ESG research, enabling the transition from committees that make qualitative judgements to ESG ratings that support consistent and transparent index decisions. Among the first SRI indices in chronological terms, the Dow Jones Sustainability World Index is also worth mentioning: introduced in 1999, it includes 2,500 leading companies worldwide in terms of sustainability performance. The FTSE Responsible Investment Indices include the Catholic Values Index, the FTSE4Good indices, the Dow Jones family of SRI indices, and the Calvert Social Index. The latter surveys 1,000 of the largest US companies based on their social audit of four criteria: the company's products, their impact on the environment, labour relations, and community relations.

Today, there are over 1,000 ESG indices, reflecting growing investor interest in ESG products and the need for metrics that accurately reflect the goals of sustainable investors. As explained by iShares (2021), the construction of an ESG index starts with the identification of a 'parent index', which defines the universe of eligible companies that can enter into the index. Second, screening is applied to remove companies from the investible universe. Moreover, the investible universe must be identified, substantially through three main approaches. The first refers to the fact that several ESG indices use exclusive screenings with reference to, for example, tobacco, firearms, or fossil fuels to avoid particular types of companies. The second approach can be traced back to the concept of 'blacklist', i.e., the exclusion of securities of companies that are positioned below a specific threshold (in the form of a score) from the point of view of environmental, social, and governance responsibility. The third approach is the one called 'Best-in-class' and therefore the selection of stocks characterised by a better ESG score than the relative indexes of the same sector or geographical area.

Moving to the choice of the components' weights, in this case the most common approach is cap-weighting: the result is that larger companies show the higher weights in the index compared to the smaller ones. Another approach used in this context is equal weighting, which assigns equal weight to all components regardless of size, while a third approach is tilting, which overweights and underweights companies based on rules related to a particular index metric. Also, in the case of ESG indices, periodic rebalancing is an opportunity to incorporate the most current ESG data.

Figure 7.3 shows a classification of sustainable investments, starting from the first form of sustainable investments based on ethics. Ethical investing is mainly based on the exclusion of specific investment themes, such as weapons, tobacco, alcohol, and pornography. The indices describing this type of investment are therefore based on the exclusion of companies operating in these sectors. Faith-based investing aims to select investments that align with their religious beliefs and values. Many faith-based investment strategies focus on ethically and socially responsible investment excluding investments that are deemed immoral. For example, a Catholic investment approach seeks equity ownership in alignment with the moral and social teachings of the Catholic Church while Islamic investing follows Sharia investment principles. Thus, indices representing faith-based investments are based on investors' religious beliefs. Focusing on ESG investing, the number and variety of indices is growing over time. Some indices target companies showing the highest ESG-rated performance in each sector of the parent index, or target companies with positive ESG characteristics while closely representing the risk and return profile of the underlying market. Finally, the most recent are the indices associated with climate investing. These indices are designed to enable investors to integrate climate risk considerations in their investment process or, in more detail, to pursue new opportunities, while aiming to align with the Paris Agreement requirements of limiting global warming to no more than 1.5 °C.

We proceed with an in-depth analysis of the characteristics of some sustainable indices of the US stock market. In particular, we have focused on the MSCI indices to allow for an easier comparison of each index against a single parent index, the MSCI USA index. The first analyses focus on the period 2013–2023, a time window in which climate indices had not yet been launched. Table 7.1 shows the description of the selected sustainable indices.

The risk-return profile of these indices can be observed in Fig. 7.4. The graph shows a similar level of risk and a slight overperformance of the following three indices: ESG Screened, ESG Focus, and the parent index. Moreover, the riskier portfolio is the MSCI Catholic Values while the worst performer is the ESG Leaders.

A further element of interest is the study of the tracking error, and its volatility, of the indices with respect to the parent index. The aim, in this case, is to verify which portfolios deviate the most, in composition, from the traditional MSCI USA Index. Figure 7.5 shows these statistics. In confirmation of the previous analysis, the indices most similar to the overall US equity market are the ESG Focus and the ESG Screened while

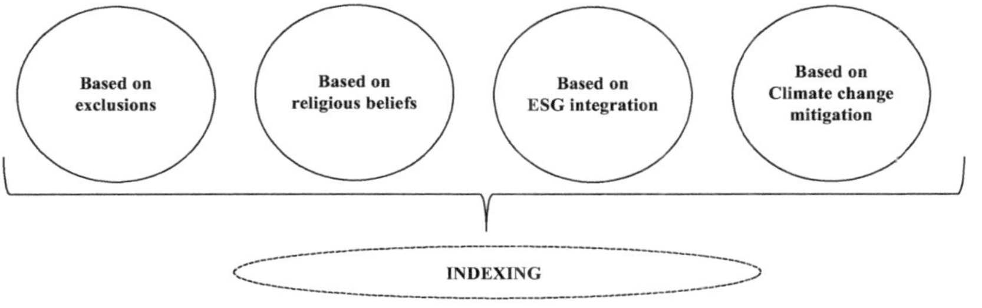

Fig. 7.3 Sustainable investing and indexation (*Source* Author's elaboration)

Table 7.1 The sample of sustainable indices: description

MSCI KLD 400 SOCIAL	Designed to provide exposure to companies with high MSCI ESG Ratings while excluding companies whose products may have negative social or environmental impacts. It consists of 400 companies selected from the MSCI USA Index
MSCI USA ESG SCREENED	Designed to exclude companies associated with controversial, civilian, nuclear weapons and tobacco that derive revenues from thermal coal and oil sands extraction or that are not in compliance with the UNGC principles
MSCI USA CATHOLIC VALUES	Designed to be aligned with the moral and social teachings of the Catholic Church
MSCI USA ESG LEADER	Target companies that have the highest ESG rated performance in each sector of the parent index
MSCI USA ESG FOCUS	Designed to target companies with positive ESG characteristics while closely representing the risk and return profile of the underlying market
MSCI USA ESG SELECT LEADERS	Designed to target companies with positive ESG factors while exhibiting risk and return characteristics similar to those of the MSCI USA Index
MSCI USA CLIMATE CHANGE ESG	Designed to enable investors to holistically integrate climate risk considerations in their investment process
MSCI USA ESG CLIMATE PARIS ALIGNED	Designed to address climate change in a holistic way by minimising its exposure to transition & physical climate risks and helping investors pursue new opportunities, while aiming to align with the Paris Agreement requirements of limiting global warming to no more than 1.5 °C
MSCI USA	Free-float weighted parent index

Source Author's elaboration on MSCI reports

those that deviate the most are the ESG Select Leaders and the Catholic Values.

The next step is the analysis of a sample composed also of two climate indices, more recently launched by MSCI, namely the MSCI USA Climate Change ESG Index and the MSCI USA Climate Paris Aligned Index. In this case, the observation period is March 2021–March 2023. The graph in Fig. 7.6 provides evidence of the tracking error statistics of the entire sample of sustainable indices. We can observe that the tracking error volatility of climate indices is significantly higher than indices based on other sustainable investing themes. Furthermore, in the case of the

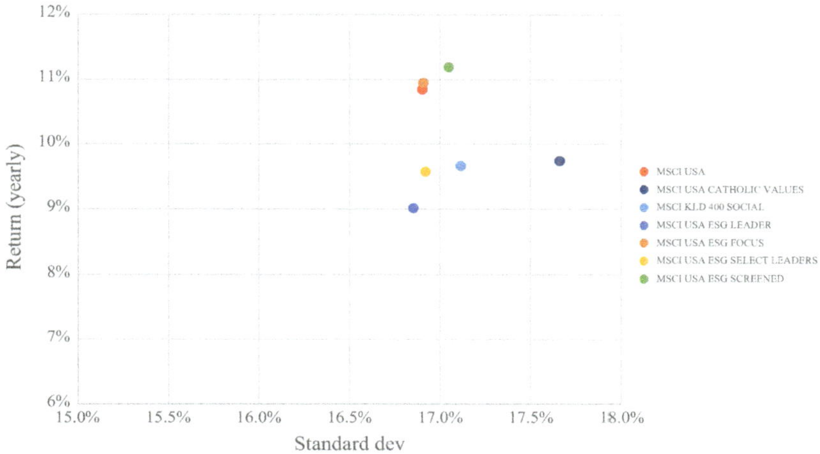

Fig. 7.4 Risk-return profile of alternative sustainable indices (2013–2023) (*Source* Author's elaboration on Bloomberg data. Analysis based on weekly returns)

Fig. 7.5 Tracking error and tracking error volatility of sustainable indices (2013–2023) (*Source* Author's elaboration on Bloomberg data. Analysis based on weekly returns)

Climate Change ESG Index we can observe a significant outperformance compared to the parent index.

Finally, we aim to verify that the tracking error of sustainable indices is driven by the size and value factors. Thus, we run the Fama–French three-factor model following the same methodology described in Chapter Four. Also in this case, the observation period is March 2021–March 2023. Table 7.2 presents the results. First, the Alpha coefficients are not significant, except in case of the ESG Focus with a negative sign, suggesting an underperformance equal to 0.41% on a yearly basis. The beta coefficients (calculated against the parent index, the MSCI USA Index) suggest a low beta nature only of the Climate Change Index. The SMB coefficient presents different signs: positive and significant in case of Catholic Value and Climate Paris Aligned, suggesting a tilt towards mid-caps. The coefficient is negative and significant in case of Climate Change, suggesting an overweight of large caps. Moreover, the HML coefficient, when statistically significant, is positive suggesting a tilt towards growth stocks if compared to the overall MSCI USA Index.

It should be emphasised that the results of the latter analysis suffer from an observation window that is too short to be able to reach solid

Fig. 7.6 Tracking error and tracking error volatility of sustainable indices (2021–2023) (*Source* Author's elaboration on Bloomberg data. Analysis based on weekly returns)

Table 7.2 Comparison between sustainable indices

	KLD 400 social	*Catholic values*	*ESG screened*	*ESG select leaders*	*ESG focus*	*ESG leaders*	*Climate change*	*climate Paris aligned*
Alpha (Ann)	0.00	0.00	0.01	0.86	(0.41)**	0.02	792.49	3.00
Market Exposure	1.01***	1.04***	1.01***	1.03***	1.01***	0.99***	0.84***	1.03***
SMB	0.03	0.09***	(0.01)	0.04*	(0.00)	(0.01)	(0.18)**	0.25***
HML	0.05**	0.11***	0.04***	0.02	(0.00)	0.03	0.15**	0.24***
R squared	0.98	0.98	0.99	0.98	0.99	0.98	0.85	0.95

Source Author's elaboration on Bloomberg data. Analysis based on weekly returns. Observation period: March 2021–March 2023

conclusions. Future research will focus on these aspects in order to be able to identify the characteristics of these innovative investment opportunities and their risk profile. Sustainable finance, and in particular that which deals with climate risk mitigation, is still in its infancy but the change underway is epochal given the convergence of the commitment of three fundamental players for its development: regulators, investors, and the asset management industry.

References

Berg, F., Koelbel, J. F., & Rigobon, R. (2022). Aggregate confusion: The divergence of ESG ratings. *Review of Finance, 26*(6), 1315–1344.

Deloitte. (2022). *Ingraining sustainability in the next era of ESG investing.* Deloitte Ireland.

Drempetic, S., Klein, C., & Zwergel, B. (2019). The influence of firm size on the ESG score: Corporate sustainability ratings under review. *Journal of Business Ethics, 167*, 333–360.

iShare. (2021). *An evolution in ESG Indexing.*

PwC Luxemburg. (2020). *2022: The growth opportunity of the century.* Sustainable Finance Series.

SustainAbility. (2020). *Rate the raters 2020: Investor survey and interview results.*

References

Amenc, N., Goltz, F., Martellini, L., & Ye, S. (2011). *Improved beta? A comparison of index-weighting schemes*. EDHEC-Risk Institute.

Albinger, H. S., & Freeman, S. J. (2000). Corporate social performance and attractiveness as an employer to different job seeking populations. *Journal of Business Ethics, 28*(3), 243–253.

Albuquerque, R., Koskinen, Y., & Zhang, C. (2019). Corporate social responsibility and firm risk: Theory and empirical evidence. *Management Science, 65*(10), 4451–4469.

Arnott, R. D., & Asness, C. S. (2003). Surprise! Higher dividends = higher earnings growth. *Financial Analysts Journal, 59*(1), 70–87.

Arnott, R. D., Hsu, J. C., & Moore, P. (2005). Fundamental indexation. *Financial Analysts Journal, 61*(2), 83–99.

Avery, C. N., & Chevalier, J. A. (1999). Herding over the career. *Economics Letters, 63*(3), 327–333.

Baker, M. (1998). Fund managers' attitudes to risk and time horizons: The effect of performance benchmarking. *The European Journal of Finance, 4*, 257–278.

Banz, R. W. (1981). The relationship between return and market value of common stocks. *Journal of Financial Economics, 9*(1), 3–19.

Bartlett, A., & Preston, D. (2000). Can ethical behaviour really exist in business. *Journal of Business Ethics, 23*, 199–209.

Berg, F., Koelbel, J. F., & Rigobon, R. (2022). Aggregate confusion: The divergence of ESG ratings. *Review of Finance, 26*(6), 1315–1344.

Bikhchandani, S., Hirshleifer, D., & Welch, I. (1992). A theory of fads, fashion, custom, and cultural change as informational cascades. *Journal of Political Economy, 100*(5), 992–1026.

E. Bolognesi, *New Trends in Asset Management*,
https://doi.org/10.1007/978-3-031-35057-3

Black, F. (1986). Noise. *The Journal of Finance, 41*(3), 528–543.

Bolognesi, E., & Burchi, A. (2023). The impact of the ESG disclosure on sell-side analysts' target prices: The new era post Paris agreements. *Research in International Business and Finance, 64*, 101827.

Bolognesi, E., & Pividori, M. (2016). Fundamental indexation in Europe: New evidence. *Journal of Financial Management, Markets and Institutions, 4*(2), 103–128.

Brown, K. C., Harlow, W. V., & Starks, L. T. (1996). Of tournaments and temptations: An analysis of managerial incentives in the mutual fund industry. *The Journal of Finance, 51*(1), 85–110.

Campbell, J. Y., & Shiller, R. J. (1988). Stock prices, earnings, and expected dividends. *The Journal of Finance, 43*(3), 661–676.

Carhart, M. M. (1997). On persistence in mutual fund performance. *Journal of Finance, 52*(1), 57–82.

Cheng, B., Ioannou, I., & Serafeim, G. (2014). Corporate social responsibility and access to finance. *Strategic Management Journal, 35*(1), 1–23.

Chevalier, J., & Ellison, G. (1997). Risk taking by mutual funds as a response to incentives. *The Journal of Political Economy, 105*(6), 1167–1200.

Chung, K. H., & Jo, H. (1996). The impact of security analysts' monitoring and marketing functions on the market value of firms. *Journal of Financial and Quantitative Analysis, 31*, 493–512.

Clarke, R. G., Krase, S., & Statman, M. (1994). Tracking errors, regret, and tactical asset allocation. *Journal of Portfolio Management, 20*(3), 16–24.

Cochran, P. L., Wood, R. A., & Jones, T. B. (1985). The composition of boards of directors and incidence of golden parachutes. *Academy of Management Journal, 28*, 664–671.

Cremers, K. M., & Petajisto, A. (2009). How active is your fund manager? A new measure that predicts performance. *The Review of Financial Studies, 22*(9), 3329–3365.

Davis, J. (2001). Mutual fund performance and manager style. *Financial Analysts Journal, 57*(1), 19–26.

Deloitte. (2022). *Ingraining sustainability in the next era of ESG investing*. Deloitte Ireland.

Devenow, A., & Welch, I. (1996). Rational herding in financial economics. *European Economic Review, 40*(3–5), 603–615. https://www.sciencedirect.com/science/article/abs/pii/0014292195000739.

De Long, J. B., Shleifer, A., Summers, L., & Waldmann, R. J. (1990). Positive feedback investment strategies and destabilizing rational expectations. *The Journal of Finance, 45*(2), 379–395.

Dhaliwal, D. S., Li, O. Z., Tsang, A., & Yang, Y. G. (2011). Voluntary nonfinancial disclosure and the cost of equity capital: The initiation of corporate social responsibility reporting. *The Accounting Review, 86*(1), 59–100.

Drempetic, S., Klein, C., & Zwergel, B. (2019). The influence of firm size on the ESG score: Corporate sustainability ratings under review. *Journal of Business Ethics, 167*, 333–360.

Dyck, A., Lins, K. V., & Pomorski, L. (2013). Does active management pay? New international evidence. *The Review of Asset Pricing Studies, 3*(2), 200–228.

Edwards, W. (1968). Conservatism in human information processing. In B. Kleinmutz (Ed.), *Formal representation of human judgement*. Wiley.

El Ghoul, S., Guedhami, O., Kwok, C. C. Y., & Mishra, D. R. (2011). Does corporate social responsibility affect the cost of capital? *Journal of Banking & Finance, 35*(9), 2388–2406.

Elton, E. J., Gruber, M. J., & Blake, C. R. (2003). Incentive fees and mutual funds. *The Journal of Finance, 58*(2), 779–804.

European Commission. (2019). *The European Green Deal*.

European Parliamentary Research Service. (2021). *Non-financial Reporting Directive*.

EY. (2021). *The future of sustainability reporting standards. The policy evolution and the actions companies can take today*.

Falkenstein, E. (1996). Preferences for stock characteristics as revealed by mutual fund portfolio holdings. *The Journal of Finance, 51*, 111–135.

Fama, E. F. (1970). Efficient capital markets: A review of theory and empirical work. *The Journal of Finance, 25*(2), 383–417.

Fama, E. F., & French, K. R. (1988). Dividend yields and expected stock returns. *Journal of Financial Economics, 22*(1), 3–25. ISSN 0304-405X, https://www.sciencedirect.com/science/article/abs/pii/0304405X88900207.

Fama, E. F., & French, K. R. (1993). Common risk factors in the returns on stocks and bonds. *Journal of Financial Economics, 33*(1), 3–56.

Fama, E. F., & French, K. R. (2010). Luck versus skill in the cross-section of mutual fund returns. *The Journal of Finance, 65*(5), 1915–1947.

Fama, E. F., & French, K. R. (2015). A five-factor asset pricing model. *Journal of Financial Economics, 116*(1), 1–22.

Fatemi, A., Glaum, M., & Kaiser, S. (2018). ESG performance and firm value: The moderating role of disclosure. *Global Finance Journal, 38*, 45–64.

Feng, J., Goodell, J. W., & Shen, D. (2022). ESG rating and stock price crash risk: Evidence from China. *Finance Research Letters, 46*. 102476.

Francis, J. R., Khurana, I. K., & Pereira, R. (2005). Disclosure incentives and effects on cost of capital around the world. *The Accounting Review, 80*, 1125–1162.

Freeman, R. E. (1984). *Strategic management: A stakeholder approach*. Cambridge University Press.

Friedman, M. (1970). A Friedman doctrine: The social responsibility of business is to increase its profits. *The New York times Magazine, 13*, 32–33.

Frino, A., & Gallaher, D. R. (2001). Tracking S&P500 index funds. *Journal of Portfolio Management, 28*(1), 44–55.

Froot, K. A., Scharfstein, D. S., & Stein, J. C. (1992). Herd on the street: Informational inefficiencies in a market with short-term speculation. *The Journal of Finance, 47*(4), 1461–1484.

Fulton, M., Kahn, B., & Sharples, C. (2012). *Sustainable investing: Establishing long-term value and performance*. Deutsche Bank Climate Change Investment Research.

Fuller, R. J. (1998). Behavioral finance and the sources of alpha. *Journal of Pension Plan Investing, 2*(3), 291–293.

Godfrey, P. C., Merrill, C. B., & Hansen, J. M. (2009). The relationship between corporate social responsibility and shareholder value: An empirical test of the risk management hypothesis. *Strategic Management Journal, 30*(4), 425–445.

Grinblatt, M., Titman, S., & Wemers, R. (1995). Momentum investment strategies, portfolio performance, and herding: A study of mutual fund behavior. *The American Economic Review, 85*(5), 1088–1105.

Grinold, R. C. (1989). The fundamental law of active management. *Streetwise: The Best of the Journal of Portfolio Management*, 161–168. https://books.google.it/books?hl=en&lr=&id=keA9DwAAQBAJ&oi=fnd&pg=PA161&dq=+grinold+law+active+management&ots=9jA3u4SKRB&sig=M0Weo52Ypy11-iUQpu3RvKVqUXA#v=onepage&q=grinold%20law%20active%20management&f=false.

He, F., Qin, S., Liu, Y., Wu, J. G. (2022). CSR and idiosyncratic risk: Evidence from ESG information disclosure. *Finance Research Letters,* 102936.

Hirshleifer, D., Subrahmanyam, A., & Titman, S. (1994). Security analysis and trading patterns when some investors receive information before others. *The Journal of Finance, 49*(5), 1665–1698.

Hoepner, A. G. F., Oikonomou, I., Sautner, Z., Starks, L. T., & Zhou, X., (2021). *ESG shareholder engagement and downside risk* (SSRN Scholarly Paper No. 2874252). Social Science Research Network.

Hsu, J. C. (2006). Cap-weighted portfolios are sub-optimal portfolios. *Journal of Investment Management, 4*(3), 1–10.

Huang, W., Luo, Y., Wang, X., & Xiao, L. (2022). Controlling shareholder pledging and corporate ESG behavior. *Research in International Business and Finance, 61*, 101655.

Ioannou, I., & Serafeim, G. (2015). The impact of corporate social responsibility on investment recommendations: Analysts' perceptions and shifting institutional logics. *Strategic Management Journal, 36*(7), 1053–1081.

iShare. (2021). *An evolution in ESG Indexing*.

Jackson, G., Bartosch, J., Avetisyan, E., Kinderman, D., & Knudsen, J. S. (2020). Mandatory non-financial disclosure and its influence on CSR: An international comparison. *Journal of Business Ethics, 162*(2), 323–342.

Jagadeesh, N., & Titman, S. (1993). Returns to buying winners and selling losers: Implications for stock market efficiency. *The Journal of Finance, XLVIII*(1), 65–91.

Jamali, D. R., El Dirani, A. M., & Harwood, I. A. (2015). Exploring human resource management roles in corporate social responsibility: The CSR-HRM co-creation model. *Business Ethics: A European Review, 24*(2), 125–143.

Jensen, M. C. (1968). The performance of mutual funds in the period 1945–1964. *The Journal of Finance, 23*(2), 389–416.

Jones, T. M. (1995). Instrumental stakeholder theory: A synthesis of ethics and economics. *Academy of Management Review, 20*(2), 404–437.

Khan, M. A. (2022). ESG disclosure and firm performance: A bibliometric and meta analysis. *Research in International Business and Finance, 61*, 101668.

Khojastehpour, M., & Johns, R. (2014). The effect of environmental CSR issues on corporate/brand reputation and corporate profitability. *European Business Review*.

Kim, Y., Park, M. S., & Wier, B. (2012). Is earnings quality associated with corporate social responsibility? *The Accounting Review, 87*, 761–796.

Kinderman, D. (2020). The challenges of upward regulatory harmonization: The case of sustainability reporting in the European Union. *Regulation & Governance, 14*(4), 674–697.

Kölbel, J. F., Busch, T., & Jancso, L. M. (2017). How media coverage of corporate social irresponsibility increases financial risk. *Strategic Management Journal, 38*(11), 2266–2284.

Lakonishok, J., Shleifer, A., & Vishny, R. W. (1992). The impact of institutional trading on stock prices. *Journal of Financial Economics, 32*(1), 23–43.

La Torre, M., Sabelfeld, S., Blomkvist, M., Tarquinio, L., & Dumay, J. (2018). Harmonising non-financial reporting regulation in Europe: Practical forces and projections for future research. *Meditari Accountancy Research, 26*, 598–621.

Lintner, J. (1965). The valuation of risky assets and the selection of risky investments in stock portfolios and capital budgets. *Review of Economics and Statistics, 47*, 13–37.

Li, Y., Gong, M., Zhang, X.-Y., & Koh, L. (2018). The impact of environmental, social, and governance disclosure on firm value: The role of CEO power. *The British Accounting Review, 50*(1), 60–75.

Luo, X., Wang, H., Raithel, S., & Zheng, Q. (2015). Corporate social performance, analyst stock recommendations, and firm future returns. *Strategic Management Journal, 36*(1), 123–136.

Malkiel, B. G. (1973). *A random walk down Wall Street*. Norton.

Malkiel, B. G. (2003). The efficient market hypothesis and its critics. *Journal of Economic Perspectives, 17*(1), 59–82.

Malkiel, B. G. (2005). Reflections on the efficient market hypothesis: 30 years later. *Financial Review, 40*(1), 1–9.

Markowitz, H. M. (1952). Portfolio selection. *Journal of Finance, 7*(1), 77–91.

Martellini, L., & Milhau, V. (2018). *Smart beta and beyond. Maximising the benefits of factor investing*. EDHEC-Risk Institute Publication.

Massa, M., & Patgiri, R. (2008). Incentives and mutual fund performance: Higher performance or just higher risk taking? *Review of Financial Studies, 21*(1), 51–99.

Mendiratta, R., Varsani, H. D., & Giese, G. (2021). How ESG affected corporate credit risk and performance. *The Journal of Impact and ESG Investing, 2*(2), 101–116.

Menkloff, L., Schmidt, E., & Brozynski, T. (2006). The impact of experience on risk raking, overconfidence, and herding of fund managers: Complementary survey evidence. *European Economic Review, 50*, 1753–1766.

Novy-Marx, R. (2012). Is momentum really momentum? *Journal of Financial Economics, 103*(3), 429–453.

Odean, T. (1999). Do investors trade too much? *American Economic Review, 89*, 1279–1298.

Pástor, L., & Stambaugh, R. F. (2012). On the size of the active management industry. *Journal of Political Economy, 120*(4), 740–781.

Piotroski, J. D. (2000). Value investing: The use of historical financial statement information to separate winners from losers. *Journal of Accounting Research, 38*, 1–41.

Plumlee, M., Brown, D., Hayes, R. M., & Marshall, R. S. (2015). Voluntary environmental disclosure quality and firm value: Further evidence. *Journal of Accounting and Public Policy, 34*(4), 336–361.

PwC Luxemburg. (2020). *2022: The growth opportunity of the century*. Sustainable Finance Series.

Roll, R. (1977). A critique of the asset pricing theory's tests part I: On past and potential testability of the theory. *Journal of Financial Economics, 14*(2), 129–176.

Roll, R., & Ross, S. A. (1984). The arbitrage pricing theory approach to strategic portfolio planning. *Financial Analysts Journal, 40*(3), 14–26.

S&P Dow Jones Indices Research. (2021). *SPIVA Scorecard report*.

Scharfestein, D. S., & Stein, J. C. (1990). Herd behavior and investment. *The American Economic Review, 80*(3), 465–479.

Sharma, V., Easterwood J. C., & Kumar, R. (2006). *Institutional herding and the internet bubble* (Working Paper Series).

Sharpe, W. F. (1964). Capital asset prices: A theory of market equilibrium under conditions of risk. *Journal of Finance, 19*(3), 425–442.

Sharpe, W. F. (1991). Arithmetic of active management. *Financial Analysts Journal, 47*(1), 7–9.

Shefrin, H. (2000). *Beyond greed and fear*. Harvard University Press.

Shefrin, H., & Statman, M. (1985). The disposition to sell winners too early and ride losers too long: Theory and evidence. *The Journal of Finance, 40*, 777–790.

Shiller, R. J. (1981). Do stock prices move too much to be justified by subsequent changes in dividends? *American Economic Review, 71*, 421–436.

Siegel, J. (2006, June 14). The noisy market hypothesis. *Wall Street Journal*, A14.

Siegel, L. B. (2003). *Benchmarks and investment management*. The Research Foundation of the Association for Investment Management and Research.

SustainAbility. (2020). *Rate the raters 2020: Investor survey and interview results*.

Trueman, B. (1988). A theory of noise trading in securities markets. *The Journal of Finance, 43*(1), 83–95.

Unerman, J. (2008). Strategic reputation risk management and corporate social responsibility reporting. *Accounting, Auditing & Accountability Journal*.

Wang, F., Mbanyele, W., & Muchenje, L. (2022). Economic policy uncertainty and stock liquidity: The mitigating effect of information disclosure. *Research in International Business and Finance, 59*, 101533.

Wong, J. B., & Zhang, Q. (2022). Stock market reactions to adverse ESG disclosure via media channels. *The British Accounting Review, 54*, 101045.

Index

E. Bolognesi, *New Trends in Asset Management*,
https://doi.org/10.1007/978-3-031-35057-3

GPSR Compliance
The European Union's (EU) General Product Safety Regulation (GPSR) is a set of rules that requires consumer products to be safe and our obligations to ensure this.

If you have any concerns about our products, you can contact us on

ProductSafety@springernature.com

In case Publisher is established outside the EU, the EU authorized representative is:

Springer Nature Customer Service Center GmbH
Europaplatz 3
69115 Heidelberg, Germany

www.ingramcontent.com/pod-product-compliance
Ingram Content Group UK Ltd.
Pitfield, Milton Keynes, MK11 3LW, UK
UKHW022222051026
15624UKWH00002B/309
* 9 7 8 3 0 3 1 3 5 0 5 6 6 *